BODY AND Soul

The Continuing Story of the Clinical Pastoral Education Movement 1992-2017

Roslyn A. Karaban, Ph.D.

Copyright © 2019 Roslyn A. Karaban, Ph.D.

Author Photo by Royal Chamberlain

All rights reserved. No part of this book may be reproduced, stored, or transmitted by any means—whether auditory, graphic, mechanical, or electronic—without written permission of the author, except in the case of brief excerpts used in critical articles and reviews. Unauthorized reproduction of any part of this work is illegal and is punishable by law.

This book is a work of non-fiction. Unless otherwise noted, the author and the publisher make no explicit guarantees as to the accuracy of the information contained in this book.

ISBN: 978-1-7325655-0-0 (sc)
ISBN: 978-1-7325655-1-7 (eBook)

Because of the dynamic nature of the Internet, any web addresses or links contained in this book may have changed since publication and may no longer be valid. The views expressed in this work are solely those of the author and do not necessarily reflect the views of the publisher, and the publisher hereby disclaims any responsibility for them.

Any people depicted in stock imagery provided by Getty Images are models, and such images are being used for illustrative purposes only.
Certain stock imagery © Getty Images.

Lulu Publishing Services rev. date: 1/8/2019

DEDICATED to the next generation of Chaplains…

Contents

Acknowledgements ix
Foreword xi
Introduction xvii
Chart xxi

Chapter 1 Clinical Pastoral Education (CPE) 1
- CPE Today 1
- Chaplaincy Today 4
- The Major Professional Chaplaincy Organizations
  and COMISS 5
  ACPE 7
  NACC 8
  NAJC (NESHAMA) 12
  APC 13
  CPSP 15
  CASC/ACSS 16
  Military Chaplains 19
  NIBIC 20
  ACCA 21
  IPFCA 22
  Muslim Chaplains Association 22
- Common Core of CPE 23

Chapter 2 Snapshots of Chaplains 25
- Descriptions of Chaplains 25
- Statistics from Major Organizations 28
  ACPE 28

	NACC 29
	NAJC/NESHAMA 30
	APC... 31
	CPSP 33
	CASC/ACSS 33
	• Chaplains: Summary 34

Chapter 3 Where and How.. 37
- Where is CPE Offered Today? 37
  Institutions.. 37
  Countries 38
  ACPE Context 41
  Broader Context... 42
  Model of Indigenization... 45
- How is CPE Taught Today? 47
  Teaching CPE: Curriculum.. 47
  Level I, Level II and Supervisory CPE................................. 48

Chapter 4 The Current Scene 49
- Recent Articles... 49
- Broadening the Conversation through Survey.................. 52
- Summary of Findings 62

Chapter 5 Reflections.. 65
- Personal Reflection 65
- Editor's Remarks... 70

Works Cited 75

Acknowledgements

In a book like this that draws upon so many different resources, there are many people to thank and I hope not to forget anyone. My thanks to my colleague John Carr who had enough faith in me to suggest my name for this project and who has been a resource throughout its writing and to Terry Bard who has been a wealth of information, a sounding board, and a phenomenal editor; to Deryck Durston, former Interim Executive Director of ACPE, who provided many years of ACPE minutes to help orient me to CPE culture and history; to my daughter Deepa who has helped me with the formatting and design for my charts and tables; to my former students (now colleagues) Kathy Cappuccio and Sue Shady who helped me understand NACC chaplaincy, and Stephanie Kelly, who together, for me, exemplify the Catholic chaplain of today;[1] to Christina Schmidt and Allison Georgia, former staff at St. Bernard's, who helped me with Survey Monkey; to my friend and colleague Irene Garrick who helped me with my survey; to the pilot group of colleagues and friends I tested

---

[1] According to NACC's website (http://www.nacc.org/certificationdefault.aspx) "The United States Conference of Catholic Bishops Subcommittee on Certification for Ecclesial Ministry and Service (formerly the USCCB Commission on Certification and Accreditation) has approved the certification standards and procedures of National Association of Catholic Chaplains for board certified chaplains and Pastoral Educators/Supervisors through 2014…Certification attests to both professional competence and endorsement for ministry by the official church." During the writing of this book, this has been extended to 2021. In future references to Catholic chaplains, it is important to know that the term "chaplain" has been officially approved by the USCCB in relation to NACC.

the survey on; and to all the people at the major chaplaincy and pastoral care organizations who answered my many emails and provided me with information and statistics: Sharon Sheflett (AAPC), Karen McCray, Trace Haythorn and John Roch (ACPE), Philip Paradowski and David Lichter (NACC), Cecile Asekoff and Gail Herman (NAJC/NESHAMA), Diane Gerard, Patricia Appelhans, Carol Pape, and Beth Stalec (APC), Toni Sedfawi, Douglas Kellough, Margaret Clark, Douglas Wilson, and Marc Doucet (CASC/ACSS), Raymond Lawrence and Brian Childs (CPSP) and Diana Dale, David Plummer and Greg Edwards (NIBIC).

As with all of my writing projects, thanks to St. Bernard's School of Theology and Ministry – my place of employment these last 30 years – which provides me with the financial, psychological and spiritual support I need. Finally, love and thanks to my family and friends – especially Prem, Deepa, Micah, Nancy, Kate, Corinne and Steph who are always there for me.

FOREWORD

I think we owe Rosyln A. Karaban considerable thanks for providing this interesting account of the continuing story of Clinical Pastoral Education and professional chaplaincy. We also need to thank Terry Bard and John Carr and the Journal of Pastoral Care and Counseling for publishing this history. Writing Body and Soul was no easy task I am sure. Rather wistfully, Dr. Karaban seems to confirm this when she came to the conclusion that the twenty-five years she was charged with for chronicling was more complicated and in many ways more convoluted than the sixty-five years her predecessor Charles Hall chronicled. Hall in Head and Heart wrote a history from the point of view of the victors, or rather, the beneficiaries of the amalgamation of several groups involved in clinical training. Hall wrote from the triumphalist perspective of the Association for Clinical Pastoral Education of which he was once executive director. Karaban, on the other hand, took the challenge of writing a history of a movement that is far more diverse and even divisive than the one Hall described.

I certainly do not want to imply that the first seven decades of clinical pastoral training was a continual flash mob singing Kumbaya. It was not. There was fierce conflict between the so-called Cabot group in Boston and the Boisen/Dunbar group in New York. There was also horrible infighting among the Southern Baptists that resulted in the graceless abandonment of a true founder of clinical training in Wayne Oates. I was Seward Hiltner's last doctoral student at Princeton and later collaborated with him on several projects before his death. Sometimes, over hamburgers at a Wendy's (he loved those burgers), he gave me accounts of the early conflicts, and some of his stories were not for the faint of heart. Hiltner anticipated some of the fractious environment we in clinical training live in now even after the formation of the Association for Clinical Pastoral Education (ACPE). He was frankly suspicious of some of the politics leading up to the formation of ACPE, and he was never very keen with the formation of the American Association of Pastoral Counselors (AAPC). He perceived that organization forfeiting its pastoral role for a secular therapeutic one. He also feared that the pastoral work of the local minister would be marginalized when the movement focuses on such specialization. Interestingly, the American Association of Pastoral Counselors (AAPC) is no longer certifying practitioners, is essentially closing up shop, and many of its certified members hold secular counselor and marriage and family therapy state licenses.

Karaban's history describes a shift in clinical pastoral movement that I do not think Hall or many others anticipated. She describes a paradigm shift that includes the movement away from a largely male dominated and largely Protestant Christian identity. The shift is also one that is moving more and more away from exclusively ordained clergy with a basic professional degree (M.Div.) to more non-ordained and a less main line ecclesial identity. Clinical training is also moving out of the hospital and is locating itself in other environments. In part this is due to the loss of support among hospital administrators in an increasingly secular society. Chaplaincy has also suffered in the need to cut hospital costs. Attempts to recover stature within medical settings are in part why many leaders within clinical pastoral training want to jettison the traditionally Judeo-Christian term 'pastoral' for the more ambiguous but more socially acceptable term 'spiritual'. Others in the movement are emphasizing data metrics and buzz words in healthcare such as 'best practices', 'benchmarks', and 'evidence based'. Many of the leading voices in this area are not specifically clinical training supervisors or practical theologians but rather sociologists, psychiatrists and MBAs! Seminary based persons, of which for a number of years I was one, saw this coming with the rather dramatic change in who was applying at denominational seminaries. There were more and more women, there were more and more second career persons, and there were more and more persons not wanting ministerial degrees but rather saw themselves as 'spiritual pilgrims' with anti-denominational inclinations. Karaban's third and fourth chapters are must reading because there she has captured the ferment in the movement that is reflective of the paradigm shift. Those two chapters are essential for understanding where the movement might want to go or where it is going no matter what. The demographic of who is involved in clinical training is in the midst of a major reconfiguration.

Dr. Karaban graciously offers a caveat in her introduction. She describes herself as an outsider to CPE but that outsider credential makes her an able objective historian. I think that she has done an excellent job of being evenhanded and as objective as an historian can be. I do think that it also limited her, somewhat, in offering a record of some of the unfortunate ferment, and in my mind needless political hostility within the movement. When I brought this observation to her and Terry Bard they suggested that I point this out and call attention to some of the *sturm und drang*. That invitation to do so is an indication of how serious and how intellectually honest Drs. Karaban and Bard are.

Body and Soul in several places indicates that there are two organizations that seem problematical for some of the leadership in clinical pastoral training. One, the College of Pastoral Supervision and Psychotherapy (CPSP) has been involved in clinical training for 27 years and its founders were involved before that within ACPE and were ACPE trained and certified. The other organization the Spiritual Care Association (SCA) rose out of a long-standing organization, the Healthcare Chaplaincy Network that was closely associated with ACPE for decades.

In 2010 there was a pivotal meeting of clinical training cognate groups in Orlando, Florida that eventually led to the development of the Common Standards and Code of Ethics. SCA did not exist in 2010 but CPSP did, and it agreed to subscribe to the Common Standards. At some point, there was some kind of vote among the other organizations. It excluded CPSP from joining. It was not a unanimous vote. Nonetheless, both CPSP and SCA are members of the COMISS Network (formerly the Coalition on Ministry in Specialized Settings) although there is no other formal relationship between CPSP and SCA and the six organizations.

In the recent past there has been outright animosity, legal posturing, and name calling. The six organizations teeter on denigrating the training and expertise of the practitioners in CPSP in particular and while CPSP recognizes the equivalence of training in ACPE, APC will only recognize one unit of CPSP training as 'counting' for the four units minimally required for certification. If Karaban or any other objective person were to compare the standards of training and the code of ethics of CPSP and ACPE, for instance, they would be hard pressed to see any difference in expectations of thoroughness, curricular integrity, and clinical and theoretical competence. SCA is raising the stakes even higher in many ways. SCA claims that its certification process which includes scientifically designed objective examinations such as used in medical school and including the observation of interviews with 'standardized patients', another tool used by medical school, is more objective and open to more scrutiny than what other organizations use. Time will tell if this claim is accurate.

So, why the animosity? One easy explanation is jobs. Particularly with the shrinking healthcare openings for well-trained chaplaincy. Competition between the organizations has become fierce. Another is personality. Both CPE and ACPE have historically had some strong personalities. When CPSP was founded, it intended to be an interest group or lobby group and remain within ACPE. That intention quickly proved to be naïve as some of the strong personalities within

ACPE saw the founders of CPSP as unfaithful to the ACPE cause and worthy of banishment to the wilderness. Whereas there have been attempts of rapprochement, they have failed in large part because of long memories and resentments that may linger. The newer organization SCA also has its strong personalities and impressive organizational skills that seem to threaten and provoke.

There is an important reason other than the competition for jobs or the clash of personalities. There really is a serious and compelling philosophical and theological difference between the organizations. Specifically, it is a difference as old as the clinical training movement itself: the difference between the goals and methods. It is a difference between a way of doing and a way of being. It is a difference between practicing on and attending to. It is a difference as old as the difference between Cabot and Boisen.

To fully understand the differences in addition to reading Hall and Karaban, one must also read Edward Thornton's Professional Education for Ministry, Allison Stokes Ministry After Freud, Robert Powell's Fifty Years of Learning Through Supervised Encounter, Brooks Holifield's A History of Pastoral Care in America, and most recently Raymond Lawrence's Recovery of Soul: A History and Memoir of the Clinical Pastoral Movement. I recommend Raymond Lawrence's Recovery of Soul in particular because Lawrence, an ACPE Supervisor, is also one of the founders and General Secretary of CPSP. His history and memoir details some of the philosophical/theological and practical differences. He is also one of those strong personalities I have mentioned along with others within both ACPE and CPSP as well SCA.

I have been naïve. I detest the internecine fighting, and I have spent a good deal of my emotional and political energy in attempting to get us to talk to each other without giving-up our identities. I have been unsuccessful, and I doubt that in my lifetime there will be any expression of honest differences while simultaneously recognizing our common and cognate missions. It would benefit us all if we did recognize our differences and commonalities. It would certainly make us look less petulant and churlish in the eyes of potential employers. The current zero sum game is self-destructive and long run.

My real hope though is, in part, with Roslyn Karaban's Body and Soul. My hope is that when this fine concise history is read, some visionaries within the movement will recognize the richness of our history and what Karaban has shown us as the actual present state of who and what chaplaincy and the training for chaplaincy is about. My hope is that those visionaries and organizers will take us to a richer movement that is faithful to pastoral care.

Brian H. Childs, Ph.D.
Professor of Bioethics and Professionalism
Director of Ethics Training
Mercer University School of Medicine
Macon and Savannah, Georgia

Introduction

When John Carr and Terry Bard first asked me to write an update to the book Head and Heart, by Charles E. Hall (1992), I thought, well, how hard can that really be? Hall wrote about seven decades of Clinical Pastoral Education (CPE) history; surely I could manage to write on the last 25 years. And yet, this has been my hardest writing project to date. It took an entire year to go through documents and articles and to come up with a framework for this history[2] and another two years to write it down.

In his Introduction to Head and Heart, Hall stated "All writing is in part autobiographical" (1992, p. xi). I would put it slightly differently. All writing is contextual, and it is important to know the writer's context that influences what s/he writes.

In many ways I am an outsider to CPE and that is part of the reason I was asked to write this book. However, some who read this book may question how I can truly know and understand the events and the culture of CPE if I have not experienced it firsthand. It is the same question that may be asked of a never-married Roman Catholic priest who does marriage counseling. Yet, it is this experience of being outside, or at least on the fringes, that enables me to observe in ways one cannot do from the inside. Sometimes it is easier to hear

---

[2] I appreciate that the term history has also been called "herstory" and since this author is female and since there has been such a large increase in women taking CPE in the last few decades, herstory may be a more appropriate term to use; however the use of the term herstory may be more distracting than it is intended to be.

the story, to be truly empathic or interpathic, if the listener's story is not too similar to the "speaker's."[3]

It's not that I never wanted to take a unit of CPE or be a certified chaplain. In my first year in seminary, I did a yearlong chaplaincy program in Boston at the Peter Bent Brigham Hospital. However, it was not a CPE program, and, at age 22, Roman Catholic, and new to this idea of ministry (this was in the 1970's), I did not even know the difference. Then, again, in the later 1970's, as I continued my studies at the doctoral level, I applied to and was accepted to do a unit of CPE at the Alta Bates Hospital in Berkeley, California. However, an internship at a pastoral counseling center became available that allowed me to continue to work at my paid secular job, and I chose to be able to eat and pay rent over pursuing CPE. In another life I would be a certified chaplain, since I loved doing hospital chaplaincy work and was told by my supervisor I was meant to be a chaplain. Of course, in another life I will also be able to sing!

In this life I have had great involvement in the pastoral care movement since the 1970's - as a Fellow in the American Association of Pastoral Counselors (AAPC) and in leadership at the Regional and Association level, as a professor of pastoral care and counseling for the last 30 years, as a member of the Society for Pastoral Theology (SPT), and, most recently, having spent four years in leadership on the SPT Steering Committee, as well as someone who taught and trained volunteer chaplains in a local volunteer hospice chaplaincy program (not CPE) for 15 years.

---

[3] I use the term empathy as to indicate the desire to listen to stories from the perspective of the speakers; as well as the ability to communicate this understanding verbally (Egan, 2010, pp. 164-167); I agree with David Augsburger that sometimes the term empathy does not go far enough and in listening interculturally a new term is necessary – interpathy (Augsburger, 1986, p.14).

Readers should know that my "living human web" [4] includes being different than the founders of CPE who were mostly male, ordained, Protestant, and ordained ministers[5]. I am female, lay, Catholic, and a professor. Yet what we all share is that we are part of the broader movement of pastoral care, counseling and chaplaincy.

Part of my assignment has been to look at trends and themes, and I have enjoyed this aspect of the research enormously. I am much more a big picture person, and identifying themes, trends, and issues is where I excel. Plodding through twenty-some years of minutes, journal articles and statistics has not been as much fun and has challenged me considerably.

The other challenge in writing this book is that in the three years it took me to write it the field of chaplaincy kept changing, and it was hard to keep up. New associations were formed, new Standards were approved, and old divisions re-emerged. This is a challenge in publication as by the time one's work is published, the material and resources are often a few years old (as they were also by the time Head and Heart was published.) At some point one has to simply put a period at the end and hope that someone else will continue the story.

It is no secret that histories are written from the perspective of those telling the stories and what they are able and willing to see and hear. All recorded histories are interpretations through a variety of lenses. This feature became clear to me one summer as I struggled to begin what I now named a daunting task of learning about and organizing twenty-plus years of documents and experiences. At that time my sister was visiting from out of town, and we were sitting on my deck. She was telling my adult children about how it was when we were growing up. She said something like this: "We were so poor when we were growing up that we ate cucumber sandwiches." I was

---

[4] Anton Boisen coined the term "living human document" (Boisen, 1971, p. 185), and this was the term that was called the "cornerstone of CPE" (Miller-McLemore, 2008, p. 3) until 1990. The term now used is "living human web" (Miller-McLemore 2008, 3) that reflects a broadening of scope to include the public arena (12).

[5] Some of the founders were physicians and academicians.

speechless and said nothing but later told my children that, although I knew we did not have a lot of money, I thought we ate cucumber sandwiches because they tasted good. My sister and I interpreted the same event through two different lenses.

I report all these experiences not so much as an apology, but to name my perspective, my lens, or my "living human web." Someone else looking at the very same documents would likely organize them differently and see things differently. Luckily, I had people who added to my perspective and translations, and who were at the core of the events of the last 25 years of CPE.

Why the title …Body and Soul? It seemed to me the most appropriate phrase to capture the shifts that have occurred since the writing of Head and Heart (Hall, 1992). This title is meant to complete the first title and propose that chaplaincy involves head, heart, body, and soul. The framework for this venture that finally made the most sense to me was common. The chapters flow from what, who, where, how, when (incorporated throughout) and wherefore. Sometimes, when in doubt, it is best to keep it simple!

SUMMARY of the HISTORY of CLINICAL PASTORAL EDUCATION
from *Head and Heart*

C O N T E X T	- Late 19th century – minister was expected to also be scholar - "Clinical pastoral education was part of a larger reform movement in theological education."(p. 5) - Church leaders such as Rev. William Palmer Ladd and physician Dr. William Keller promoted more practical education for ministers. They initiated a clinical program developed under Joseph Fletcher at Episcopal Divinity School (EDS) in Cambridge, MA, which was another precursor of CPE - Development of psychology in the early 20th century (William James, Sigmund Freud), which focused on the experiences of individuals - In the field of education, John Dewey stressed the experiential side of learning - Changes and conversations taking place in the fields of law, medicine, science and religion in Europe and America - Elwood Worcester formed a clergy-physician clinic at Emmanuel Church in Boston - beginning of Emmanuel Movement, a precursor of CPE and the pastoral counseling movement
	Primary founders of CPE movement: Richard Cabot & Anton Boisen
R I C H A R D C A B O T	- Wealthy Unitarian layman, physician, professor at Harvard, founder of medical social work - Creator of clinical pathological conferences - Saw need to go beyond symptoms to causes - Taught a course with Worcester (physician) dealing with minister's work with sick and dying and recommended clinical year for seminary students - Taught a course on case study method at Harvard Medical School that Anton Boisen attended in 1922 just after release from psychiatric stay - Cabot facilitated Boisen in beginning clinical training, later called CPE - Emphasized need for supervised experience in application of theology in pastoral care

A N T O N B O I S E N	- "The father of clinical pastoral education" (Hall, 1992, p. 8)
- Recovering from mental illness, initiated clinical training in 1925
- Received counseling from Elwood Worcester
- Early students: Philip Guiles, Carroll Wise, Seward Hiltner, Helen Flanders Dunbar, Russell Dicks, Rollin Fairbanks, and Granger Westberg
- Called case study approach learning from "living human documents"
- Tried to integrate intellectual and emotional aspects of life
- Emphasized need to study theology by seeking to understand religious experiences of people

PIONEERS

Helen Flanders Dunbar
- Integrated her backgrounds in philosophy, psychiatry and theology
- Worked with Cabot
- Promoted holistic view
- Viewed symbolism as bond between theologians and psychiatrists
- Emphasized interrelatedness of intellect and emotions
- Medical director of Council for Clinical Training (incorporated in 1930)
- Director of Joint Committee on Religion in Medicine
- Leader of New England Branch

Carroll Wise
- Trained with Boisen
- Stayed at Worcester State Hospital for 12 years – changed emphasis from research to pastoral
- Emphasized integration of intellect and emotion
- Clashed with Hiltner - said he wasn't rooted deeply enough in emotional life
- Supervisor to Dicks and Fairbanks who became leaders in New England group

Russell Dicks
- Interested in ministering to physically ill
- Chaplain at Mass General Hospital
- Created the verbatim
- Wrote The Art of Ministering to the Sick with Cabot (1936)

Austin Philip Guiles
- Trained at Worcester (1928), Mass General (1930)
- Director of Clinical Training at Andover Newton Theological School (ANTS) (1931)
- First professor of clinical training at theological school

Seward Hiltner
- … "may have done more to spread intellectual understanding of pastoral care, pastoral theology, pastoral psychology, and clinical pastoral education than any other person." (p. 29)
- Disciple of Bosien; also worked with Dunbar and Wise
- Emphasized insight more than method
- Became member of NY group
- Founded Pastoral Psychology (with Doniger) and wrote Preface to Pastoral Theology

S P L I T	• Split in 1930s among pioneers precipitated by Boisen's second psychotic episode. Boisen became enamored with and pursued two women – Alice Batchelder and Helen Dunbar. His mother, whom he adored, died in 1930. All of this led to a psychotic break, and Cabot hospitalized Boisen. Cabot wanted Boisen gone and Guiles supported Cabot. Cabot believed that as a rule, mental illness was incurable. The split was both personal and philosophical. • Boisen supported and criticized both groups		
	Institute of Pastoral Care		Council for Clinical Training
N E W E N G L A N D G R O U P	• More conservative: focus on preserving past and present values, beliefs and methods • Believed clinical training should be an integral part of theological education and that theological schools should have a significant role in the movement • Emphasis on student-patient relationship • More of emphasis on head over heart • Called pastor "shepherd of the soul" • Dicks, Cabot, Guiles, leaders, followed by Fairbanks, Johnson, Burns, Strunk, Billinsky and Smith • Cabot – focused on application of theology in pastoral care • Students learned from failure, used verbatims, growing edges • In general, slower to embrace psychological understanding	**N E W Y O R K G R O U P**	• Radical – going to root and seeking abrupt and far-reaching change • Pastoral competence comes from psychodynamic insight • Emphasized standards for accreditation • Study of living human documents, unconscious, psychiatric hospitals, verbatim and case studies • Emphasis on pastoral skill • Called pastor "physician of the soul" • Dunbar wanted physicians as part of program • Dunbar, Wise, Hiltner and Beatty, followed by Bruder, Bigham, Kuether, Rice and Preston • Emphasis on pastoral skill • Thought that students needed to understand their own emotions and have psychological understanding of persons to whom they ministered • Instead of advanced theological degrees, supervisors entered psychoanalytic therapy • Focus on depth of psychological understanding

D E V E L O P M E N T S	- First National Conference on Clinical Training, June 6-7, 1944, Western Theological Seminary, Pittsburgh, PA – crystallization of clinical pastoral education as a movement: "If a single event were to be designated as the point in time when clinical pastoral education became a movement, it would be the first National Conference on Clinical Training" (p. 49) - 1946: College of Chaplains – division of American Protestant Health Association – organized in the tradition of the New England group - 1947: Institute of Pastoral Care – published Journal of Pastoral Care - 1948: Association of Mental Health Hospital Chaplains – related to American Psychiatric Association – in tradition of New York group - In 1940s and 50s community of correctional chaplains developed – American Correctional Chaplains Association and American Protestant Correctional Chaplains Association
U N I F I C A T I O N	- 1950s: The Committee of 12- foundation for unified CPE -1951 (Institute of Pastoral Care, Council for Clinical Training, Lutherans) - 1950's – 6 national conferences - 1960s: Unification of the CPE movement - 1960s: formation of American Association of Pastoral Counselors (AAPC) "as a direct outgrowth of the Clinical Pastoral Education Movement." (p. 67) - 1960s: joint activities of Council for Clinical Training and Institute of Pastoral Care - In the beginning, majority of AAPC members were also members of Association of CPE - 1967: ACPE becomes a legal entity; Executive Director John Smith; 1968-1984 Charles Hall, Executive Director
D I V E R S I T Y	- 70's and 80's: Unity of spirit/diversity of expression - 9 Regions formed - Until 1970's, not many women in CPE; meeting of women at national meeting of ACPE in 1974 - 1980 – few African Americans – task force formed – REM Racial/Ethnic Minorities in CPE – George Polk - Inclusivity broadening: conservative, evangelical, gays and lesbians, Jews - NACC formed 1965 - International developments: Canada, Netherlands, Australia, New Zealand, Philippines, Singapore - Coming together of all pastoral care, pastoral counseling, church agencies and CPE organizations in a Congress on Ministry in Specialized Settings (COMISS) - International Pastoral Care and Counseling Movement - Dialogue 88 held in Minneapolis, MN - NAJC formed 1990

CHAPTER ONE

Clinical Pastoral Education (CPE)

Clinical Pastoral Education (CPE) Today: What is it?

Since this book is about the continuing story of CPE, it would be helpful at the outset to identify a contemporary definition of the movement and methodology. According to Joan Hemenway,

> Clinical Pastoral Education (CPE) is an educational methodology that combines knowledge of psychology (who we are) with knowledge of theology (what we believe) with process education (how we learn) in order to prepare seminarians, clergy and qualified lay people to provide effective interfaith spiritual care amidst the religious and social complexities of the world. (Hemenway, 2005, p.323)

What has changed in this definition since the publication of *Head and Heart* (Hall, 1992)? The re-emphasis on theology, the addition of qualified laity, the shift to interfaith rather than inter-denominational care, and the emphasis on the social contexts are immediately evident.

What may not be quite as evident in Hemenway's definition, but remains certainly part of her contribution to the field, is the shift from personal and individual care, which drew heavily on psychoanalytic and humanistic theories, to a broader framework that includes both the individual and the systemic, that draws also on systems-centered theories.

One consistent description of CPE throughout the years is that it is regarded as a movement. Charles Hall used this term to describe the history of CPE, and it is the word that leaders in the field like Homer Jernigan (2000) continued to use. Peter VanKatwyck (2000) described the CPE movement by using the terms "chapters," "shifts," and "seasons" – from what to do (1925-1935), to what to know, (1935-1945) to what to say (1945-1955), and to what to be (1955-1965) (p. 243). He extended this description to the 1970s and added family systems theory and the self being viewed in relation to social context, and the 1980s with postmodern theories and the self-emerging through social discourse covering the years beyond the 1980s, that would suggest that today CPE incorporates all of the above and represents an integration of what came before with the addition of what the last 25 years have yielded.

Another current definition of CPE comes from the University of Rochester, NY Strong Memorial Hospital website[6]:

> Our Clinical Pastoral Education (CPE) Program is a comprehensive program that integrates peer review, supervisory evaluation, and personal reflection. As a

---

[6] Other descriptions were similar. From Minnesota/St Paul: Expect to be involved in ministry, to learn about yourself, to be in conversation with others, learn about your limp (Jacob and angel) and to be encouraged and challenged. http://www.allinahealth.org/ahs.cpe.nst/page/cpe_programs
From the Carolinas Health Care System: professional training for clergy and laity; ministry and reflection; pastoral identity, authority and functioning; integration http://www.carolinashealthcare.org/clinical-pastoral-education-programs. Many more could be cited that would be similar.

student in our program, your learning will be facilitated through intense involvement with persons in need, feedback from peers and teachers, and closely guided personal and theological reflection. This action-reflection model of learning will help you to develop a new awareness of yourself and those to whom you minister. Plus, as part of an interdisciplinary team, you will apply learned theory with your own personal and pastoral experience as you minister to patients, families, and staff. You will be encouraged to use your own personal experience as a resource for ministry. Your learning will be enhanced through active participation in educational conferences, interdisciplinary meetings, and grand rounds. (http://www.urmc.rochester.edu/chaplaincy/CPE/programs.cfm)

CPE emphasizes education and supervision: "Clinical Pastoral Education is interfaith professional education for ministry. It brings theological students and ministers of all faiths (pastors, priests, rabbis, imams and others) into supervised encounter with persons in crisis." (http://S51162813.onlinehome.us/faq/)

Whereas, in the past, the primary students enrolled in CPE programs were seminary or post-seminary students, it is no longer a requirement that one has seminary experience to partake in a Level I unit of CPE. In order to participate in a CPE residency (4-unit program), some programs require that applicants be currently or formerly enrolled in graduate theological or related studies. Many students take a Level I unit of CPE as part of their seminary education, and a number of denominations require a basic unit in order to be ordained. Other students, however, take a Level I unit of CPE as part of discerning where their gifts lie.

Roslyn A. Karaban, Ph.D.

Chaplaincy Today

The most basic definition of chaplaincy is the work/ministry conducted by a chaplain. Colloquially, a chaplain is defined as: the minister in charge of the chapel; a minister officially attached to the military or an institution; or a minister appointed to assist a bishop (Merriam-Webster.com.2017). For the purpose of this book, a chaplain is defined as a spiritual leader that is officially attached to an institution such as a hospital, long-term care facility, hospice agency, prison or jail, university, the military or veterans' facilities. In particular, most of the chaplaincy considered relative to CPE is chaplaincy taking place in a hospital or medical center. It is significant that the institution names the office of the chaplain and determines what those serving in that office are to be called. [7] Whereas, in the past, the common term for the discipline was chaplaincy provided by a chaplain, more recently, within the last 25 years, these same offices have also been called Pastoral Care Departments and Spiritual Care Departments. What the chaplain is called has great significance. This designation will be addressed in the next chapter. In this chapter, the terms chaplain and chaplaincy will be used since they are common within the major organizations that certify professional chaplains. Chaplains at hospitals primarily provide pastoral/spiritual care to patients, families, and staff through visitation and may also be responsible for worship services and may be called upon for emergency experiences such as traumas, deaths, baptisms, giving communion, performing weddings, leading memorial services and other ceremonial and sacramental activities.

---

[7] A 1997 Vatican document states that the word chaplain is reserved for the ordained, Instruction on Certain Questions Regarding the Celebration of the Nonordained Faithful in the Sacred Ministry of Priests," (1997, 403). The US Catholic Bishops did not accept this document and it is the institution – hospital, prison, school – that decides the name the chaplain is to be called. This is more of an issue for Catholics than Protestants as most Protestant chaplains continue to be ordained ministers.

The Major Professional Chaplaincy Organizations and COMISS

The Network on Ministry in Specialized Settings (COMISS)

The beginnings of COMISS can be traced to the 1920's in action-reflection ministry for seminarians (Midwest – inner city – 1923) and in the general and psychiatric hospital (1920s – New England), but not formalized until 1988. COMISS was and is part of the larger pastoral care movement and as such was and is affected by what goes on in its constituencies as well as by what is taking place locally, domestically, and globally. Thus, what is referred to as the "incoherence" in the pastoral care movement in the 1920s affected and made an impact on the beginnings of COMISS. This incoherence also contributed to what Edward Thornton referred to as the incoherence of clinical training being a reaction against traditional seminary education, but one that was at the periphery of seminary life, and thus without a power base (Thornton, 1970, p. 24). This incoherence and lack of power base continued into the 1990s where this book picks up its history. In 1993 COMISS included a membership of 25 religious endorsing bodies, 12 pastoral care, counseling, chaplaincy and education organizations, three organizations providing ministry in specialized settings, and seven organizations listed as "other." John Gleason cited this membership category as one example of the continuance of the theme of "incoherence" (Gleason, 1993, pp. 118-119). Another example of incoherence would be that in the Dictionary of Pastoral Care and Counseling (1990), a pivotal work in the field of pastoral care, there is no entry for the term COMISS and only one mention of the original Council on Ministry in Specialized Settings.

In the 1960s five national health care associations met together and agreed to meet annually. In 1978 this group voted to found a Council on Ministry in Specialized Settings. In 1988 this Council became a Congress and inaugural documents were signed. COMISS was founded with principles of coordination, cooperation, and collaboration among organizations, while maintaining the autonomy of each organization. The dream of the 1960s, 1970s, and 1980s became a reality in 1988 with the legal formation of COMISS, but there was a "widening credibility gap" (Gleason, 1993, p. 120) between leaders and members who resisted the process of institutionalization. This gap is reflected in the meeting of The College of Pastoral Supervision and Psychotherapy in 1992 when the Secretary to the Governing Body accused the pastoral care movement of supporting institutionalization.

Dialogue 88 – a combined national meeting when COMISS was officially launched - was a high moment in COMISS history with the coming together of more than 1900 attendees from most major pastoral care groups. However, a lull followed this meeting and the excitement surrounding the event dwindled. COMISS commissioned the Alban Institute to assess this shift, and Alban's consultant reported the findings at the 1990 COMISS assembly. This consultant made a number of recommendations to clarify, refine, assess and respond to the COMISS project. By 1991 an air of optimism returned, although there was still great diversity of opinion about the COMISS mission, meaning, and vision. A formal instrument was conducted in 1992 in an attempt to determine if there still existed a gap between members and leaders regarding vision and outcome possibilities. This study concluded "COMISS's greatest challenge is to increase coherence by affirming, articulating, and expediting a clear vision and strategy for more effective ministry to persons in special need at the systems level." (Gleason, 1993, p. 126)

Today, COMISS is known as The Network on Ministry in Specialized Settings, or The COMISS Network. The COMISS website describes The COMISS Network as "the product of many years of interfaith cooperation in the development and delivery of pastoral services in a variety of specialized ministry settings" (such as chaplaincies in healthcare and pastoral counseling, CPE mental health settings, the armed forces, business and industrial settings, correctional institutions, and the Department of Veterans Affairs. The website states that COMISS Network is a "forum for dialogue and action" (http://comissnetwork.org/) for:

- Professional Accreditation and Certifying Organizations
- Religious Endorsing Bodies
- Professional Pastoral Care Organizations
- Chaplain and Pastoral Counselor Employer Organizations

Currently, COMISS Network Initiatives include Pastoral Care Week and CCAPS, the COMISS Commission for Accreditation of Pastoral Services.

The Association for Clinical Pastoral Education (ACPE)

According to its website, ACPE, founded in 1967, was established in 1967 as a merger of the following four organizations in the clinical pastoral education movement: Council for Clinical Training of Theological Students, Institute of Pastoral Care, Inc., Lutheran Advisory Council on Pastoral Care and Southern Baptist Association of Clinical Pastoral Education. Today (2015) it is "a multicultural, multifaith organization devoted to providing education and improving the quality of ministry and pastoral care offered by spiritual care givers of all faiths" (http://www.acpe.edu/?m=2518). Much of the history of how this organization formed and developed is addressed in Head and Heart (Hall, 1992).

The current mission statement (2015) of ACPE is: "Advancing exceptional experience-based theological education and professional practice to heal a hurting world" and the vision statement is:

> We will be an organization where people of diverse
> faith traditions, backgrounds, and cultures collaborate

to provide innovative experiential education. We will lead in the theory and practice of clinical education for spiritual care. We will promote and broaden the provision of quality professional theological education in a variety of settings. (http://s531162813.onlinehome.us/about/mission-and-vision-html)

According to its website, (http://s531162813.online.us/about), there are now more than 2300 members, 300 accredited ACPE Centers, and 600 certified faculty members (Supervisors).

ACPE certifies Supervisors but not chaplains. The classification categories of Professional Chaplain or Certified Supervisor are other ways of defining chaplaincy and advancing chaplaincy to higher levels and standards of practice. ACPE provides this education through Level II CPE units or CPE residencies (4 units). The most significant differences in the last 20-25 years of chaplaincy, ACPE, and other chaplaincy organizations include enhancing chaplain professionalization, increasing training requirements (including the required number of units of CPE), and the expectation that in order to be a chaplain one must have fulfilled more training and practice requirements. Another difference is that although the program and requirement of conducting CPE through approved centers/programs unite all certifying organizations, each association attracts its own constituencies in the context of its own mission each providing its own certifying body. Certification qualifications have evolved considerably in the last 25 years. A brief description of the other major chaplain organizations follows.

The National Association of Catholic Chaplains (NACC)

The NACC was founded in 1965, two years before the Council for Clinical Training and the Institute for Pastoral Care merged formally establishing ACPE in 1967. The CPE movement had been in existence since the 1920's, and, according to Hall, "ACPE accepted

Catholic women in CPE programs before the time they were accepted as members in NACC." (Hall, 1992, p. 172). Although this statement is accurate, the women who were accepted were women religious (sisters), and although women religious are actually laywomen, both Roman Catholics and Protestants view them as something in between the clergy and laity.[8] NACC began accepting lay people (non-ordained, non-religious) as early as 1975 (Accardi, 2005, p. 1). Significant for Roman Catholics and CPE in the last two decades is not just the presence of Roman Catholic women as chaplains, but the predominance of Roman Catholic laity taking CPE programs and seeking certification by NACC. As of May 2015, the total number of certified members in NACC was 1482 (970 female and 512 male) that included: 784 laypeople (533 female and 215 male); 393 women religious; and 305 ordained (254 priests, 9 brothers, and 42 deacons). (D. Lichter, Executive Director, NACC, personal communication, May 13, 2015)

Historically, the initial relationship between ACPE and NACC was simultaneously described as both "complementary" and "competitive" (Hall, 1992, p. 172). Early on, NACC did not adopt the ACPE programs although it borrowed what was considered to be helpful. NACC began with basics and added components over time. This operational difference in requirements created tension with ACPE (Hall, 1992, p. 174). In the 1980's many Catholics were dually certified both as ACPE supervisors, and, then, as NACC supervisors with additional Catholic studies. This difference became pivotal in the 1990s and 2000s.

By 2007, the requirements for NACC supervisory certification

---

[8] For example, membership in AAPC for Catholics was restricted to priests and sisters (women religious) who fit into the definition of "minister" – "a person who has been authorized by a denomination or faith group through ordination, consecration or equivalent means" (AAPC application, 1992) even though laity were educationally and clinically qualified to become members. The other factor here is that until the 1980's, it was primarily women religious who were getting the education and training necessary to join NACC, AAPC or ACPE.

were comparable to those of Association of Professional Chaplains (APC). NACC chaplain certification now requires four units of CPE; ACPE requires 4 units to become a clinical member. Roman Catholics certified by ACPE enjoy reciprocity and have the additional ability to demonstrate personal, professional, and Roman Catholic competencies (from website FAQ). According to the ACPE website, agreements between ACPE and NACC accept the student unit credits of each other's organization. (http://acpe.edu/WhoWeAreRR.html) NACC does not have accredited CPE centers. The United States Conference of Catholic Bishops Commission on Certification and Accreditation (USCCB/CCA) accredited CPE centers, and when it closed at the end of 2011, it no longer accredited centers. Most USCCB/CCA accredited centers were already ACPE accredited centers. The few remaining USCCB/CCA accredited centers have become or are in the process of becoming ACPE accredited centers.

NACC supervisors were able to supervise in ACPE programs under certain conditions. The NACC Board of Directors decided at its May 2012 meeting to no longer train for CPE supervisor certification, nor certify new CPE supervisors, while continuing to offer renewal of certification as CPE supervisors for those who desire to maintain that certification. Recognition processes for NACC supervisors to be ACPE certified and ACPE supervisors to be NACC certified were refined, and put in place. All NACC certified supervisors are now dually certified with ACPE.[9] The relationship between ACPE and NACC is now best described as mostly complementary and reciprocal.

A Roman Catholic certifying body is best prepared to focus on the unique importance of the Roman Catholic identity, knowledge, and competency within chaplaincy, particularly the uniqueness of

---

[9] This section was greatly enhanced and partly written by David Lichter, current Executive Director of NACC.

being a Catholic lay ecclesial[10] minister. Including Roman Catholics in ACPE has always been part of CPE history, but the initial emphasis was on ordained priests and women religious. With the increasing number of Catholic laity getting theological degrees, becoming board certified with NACC, and pursuing careers in chaplaincy, the field of chaplaincy in Catholic health care institutions, began to shift in the early 1980's. Most pastoral care departments in Catholic hospitals now have lay people on staff, whereas many Protestant chaplains of varying denominations are still ordained. Those lay Catholics wishing to achieve national certification in NACC, take four units of training and obtain a graduate theological degree to satisfy the Common Standards' academic qualification to become board certified (QUA 3 – a graduate-level theological degree from a college, university or theological school accredited by a member of the Council for Higher Education Accreditation). Another factor in this lay ministry phenomenon is that many lay Catholics going into ministry are 50 years and older, and the majority of lay ministers going into chaplaincy work are women. Therefore, there are older, married, lay, Catholic women trying to fit into what has as its foundations, younger, single and married, ordained, or preparing to be ordained, Protestant men, and later, women. One can see where the Protestant and Catholic cultures have been colliding.

---

[10] The term "lay ecclesial ministers/ministries" has been in existence for the last two decades. Most recently the USCCB (United States Conference of Catholic Bishops) in their 2005 document "Co-Workers in the Vineyard of the Lord: A Resource for Guiding the Development of Lay Ecclesial Ministry," identified in a generic way "lay ecclesial ministries" many different leadership positions in parishes, schools, diocesan agencies, and Church Institution (p.5).

Roslyn A. Karaban, Ph.D.

NESHAMA: Association of Jewish Chaplains (formerly known as NAJC)[11]

Jewish chaplains served in the military since the Civil War. In the late 19th century there were scattered numbers of Jewish chaplains in prisons and hospitals. The professional field of Jewish chaplaincy did not formally emerge until the 1980s when mostly rabbis started pursuing careers in chaplaincy and taking additional training in CPE. Spearheaded by Rabbis Jeffrey Silberman, Charles Spirn, and Terry Bard, discussions began to emerge about forming an organization for Jewish chaplains. The National Association of Jewish chaplains (NAJC) was founded in 1990 at a conference in Atlantic City. According to the NAJC website (http://www.najc.org/about/history) today there are 300 professional members and an additional 300 supporters (lay people, congregational rabbis, students and Israeli affiliates). NAJC professional chaplains serve in geriatric centers, hospices, hospitals, prisons, community, mental health facilities, and the military and in training and teaching pastoral care.

In the last 25 years there have been significant developments in NAJC. In 1993 rabbis, cantors, and laity alike, with chaplaincy training, and evidence of advanced Jewish and secular education could become full professional members. This shift is similar to what took place in NACC. In 1995 a program of certification was required and provided more professional training. In 2013 (according to its website – exact numbers given in next chapter) there are now 100 certified Jewish chaplains that hold the credential of Board Certified Chaplain (BCC). In 2004 NAJC joined with other pastoral care organizations to establish common standards for ethics,

---

[11] According to Cecille Asekoff, Executive Vice President of NESHEMA, NAJC's name was changed to NESHAMA because "we wanted to have a Hebrew term as part of our name while at the same time maintaining the initials NAJC which most people know us as" (C. Asekoff, personal communication, August 14, 2014) (Neshama means soul). The organization's name changed during the writing of this book and both titles are used.

education and certification. This new group is called the Spiritual Care Collaborative. Finally, since 2005, NAJC has played a role in Israel's focus on spiritual care. Israeli delegates attend NAJC conferences and there is collaboration among individuals and groups in the US, Canada, and Israel.

NAJC has various levels of membership. To become a regular member one must: be an ordained or invested Rabbi, Cantor or Jewish lay professional; have advanced Jewish education, four units of CPE chaplaincy training, at least a Bachelor's degree, be a member for at least 12 consecutive months, fulfill NAJC certification requirements, have a certification number, and meet annual continuing educational requirements.

Association of Professional Chaplains (APC)

A fourth major professional chaplaincy organization is the Association of Professional Chaplains (APC). APC traces its history back to the summer of 1942 and the vision of Rev. Russell L. Dicks, who in 1946, invited hospital chaplains to meet with him at the annual meeting of the American Protestant Hospital Association (APHA) in Philadelphia. From this first meeting of 16, the Association of Protestant Hospital Chaplains was formed and Dicks served as the first President.

As Chair of the APHA Commission to Study Religious Work in Hospitals, Dicks learned that in 1940 only 18 general hospitals had full-time chaplains. By 1945 this number had increased to 38 representing only 8% of the 465 hospitals that responded to a survey. By 1946 a Chaplain's section of APHA was organized and Chaplain Leicester Potter, President, saw the need for standards and certification. By 1950 standards were adopted that included 2 units of CPE.

In the 1960s APHC was renamed Chaplain's Division of the APHA, growing in independence from APHA. In 1968 the Chaplain's Division was renamed the College of Chaplains. Membership grew to 500 in 20 years, and, after changing its name to College of Chaplains

(COC), membership grew to 900 within a brief 4-year span. As the COC grew it was able to hire a part-time executive director and to enhance its standards for certification. ACPE became the primary provider for the clinical training required for certification.

The Association of Mental Health Chaplains (AMHC) also emerged in the 1940s (1946). This group expanded, and by 1968, it certified Catholic, Jewish and Protestant chaplains with CPE being the common training requirement; in the early 1970s changed its name to the Association of Mental Health Clergy. At that time, it was unique by its expansive inclusion of non-Christian members.

In the 1960s women sought chaplaincy certification, and, in the 1970s Catholic sisters began to apply for certification as well. Military chaplains who served in hospitals and medical facilities joined. AMHC experienced a decline in membership, and in 1993 it joined with the College of Chaplains. In 1998 this collaboration reincorporated itself to become the organization now known as the Association of Professional Chaplains (APC). Around this same time (1996) the College of Chaplains separated from APHA and became independent. Part of this move was a move not only toward independence but a move toward becoming more interfaith and intercultural.[12]

According to its website (http://www.professionalchaplains.org/content.asp?contentid=24) APC has 4000 member chaplains and affiliates (see next chapter for exact numbers). These four organizations – ACPE, NACC, NAJC and APC – in addition with AAPC (American Association of Pastoral Counselors) and CAPPE (Canadian Association for Pastoral Practice and Education) have agreed on Common Standards for Professional Chaplains, Supervisors and Codes of Ethics.

---

[12] Thanks to Carol Pape, Chief Operating Officer of the Association for Professional Chaplains, for reviewing this section for accuracy.

Body and Soul

The College of Pastoral Supervision and Psychotherapy (CPSP)

According to John Gleason, the formation of The College of Pastoral Supervision and Psychotherapy (CPSP) was a response to the loss of the original CPE paradigm and the supervisory characteristics and experiences (1998, p. 4). CPSP was founded in 1990 to recover the "spirit" of CPE. Gleason (1998) described CPSP as:

> ...a certifying body of clinical supervisors, pastoral counselors, and pastoral psychotherapists whose particular competence lies in the integration of theology and behavioral sciences, with particular allegiance to the two phrases that are associated with CPSP are 'recovery of soul' and 'development of idiosyncratic self'.

In 2001 Raymond J. Lawrence, General Secretary, CPSP, described CPSP in this way:

> CPSP was formed out of the memories of our own experience in clinical training...We remembered the redemptive process of our own clinical training... as transformative ...[and] constructed the Chapter model...as the best hope for fostering continuing transformation... (Lawrence 2001, 3)

According to their website (http://www.pastoralreport.com/covenant.html, CPSP members agree to a covenant that begins:

> We, the CPSP members see ourselves as spiritual pilgrims seeking a truly collegial professional community. Our calling and commitments are, therefore, first and last theological. We covenant to address one another and to be addressed by one another in a profound theological sense. We commit to being

mutually responsible to one another for our professional work and direction.

The Standards (2013) state that CPSP offers programs in CPE/CPT (Clinical Pastoral Education/Training), Pastoral Psychotherapy, Pastoral Counseling and Clinical Chaplaincy (p. 1). CPSP claimed a model of governance different from that of ACPE. Instead of a centralized government, CPSP operates in geographic Chapters (6-12 members). CPSP credentials members to work in hospitals, hospices, counseling centers, seminaries, churches, seminaries and psychotherapy offices. CPSP certifies Diplomate in CPE/CPT Supervision, Diplomate in Pastoral Psychotherapy, Board Certified Clinical Chaplain, Board Certified Associate Clinical Chaplain, Pastoral Counselor, Associate Pastoral Counselor, Hospice/Palliative Care, and Clinically Trained Minister (p. 11). CPSP has more than 1000 credentialed members. CPSP also accredits a wide range of training programs in CPE, pastoral counseling, and pastoral psychotherapy. CPSP and ACPE have been at odds with each other and have been in a competitive, sometimes contentious relationship. This relationship continues to evolve as does CPSP.[13]

The Canadian Association for Spiritual Care (CASC)/Association canadienne de soins spirituels (ACSS)

CASC (Canadian Association for Spiritual Care)/ACSS (Association canadienne de soins spirituels) is: "a multifaith organization, committed to the professional education, certification and support of people involved in spiritual care, pastoral counseling, education and research." (http://www.spiritualcare.ca/index.asp)

CASC/ACSS was organized in 1965 as CCSPE (Canadian

---

[13] During the final editing of this chapter I received notice that in August 2015 CPSP is undergoing revisions in their certification process. Also during the writing of this book, a spin-off group - The Center for Spiritual Care and Pastoral Formation – was formed. Thanks to Brian Childs, President of CPSP for reviewing this section.

Council for Supervised Pastoral Education) with a constitution and by-Laws. Archibald MacLaughlin was elected the first president and Dean Charles Fielding as Chair of the National Accreditation and Certification (A&C) Committee. In 1966 standards and procedures for certification were adopted that had many elements in common with American standards of the day with the hope of negotiating reciprocity with ACPE in the future. Currently, certification remains an important component of the organization's function.

Because CPE had its roots in the United States, many Canadians experienced their first CPE units and/or residencies in the U.S. during the 1930s, 40s, and 50s. Men such as Albert Bentum, Earle McKnight, Archie MacLaughlin and Charles Taylor were among the first to do so. In 1951, Earle McKnight supervised Charles Taylor as he conducted a unit of CPE at the Victoria General Hospital in Halifax, Nova Scotia. This inaugural program was followed by the generation of a unit in Hamilton, Ontario with Archie MacLaughlin and Jack Breckenridge in 1952. In 1958, due to the efforts of Charles Fielding, The Institute of Pastoral Training (IPT) was incorporated in Toronto.

In 1967, Murray Thompson offered an accredited unit of CPE at the Vancouver General Hospital. In 1969 Bryan Pearce offered the first accredited CPE Unit in Quebec, and, in 1972, Herb Briethaupt was hired as the first paid Executive Officer. The 1970's saw a proliferation of programs across Canada.

1973 was a critical year as discussions were undertaken with AAPC for reciprocity for PCE (Pastoral Care Education) trained supervisors and practitioners and new standards were trialed for a new category of Specialist: Pastoral Counselors, Clinically Trained Pastors and Chaplains. Final approval of the Specialist standards passed in 1975. Prior to this, only CPE and PCE Supervisors were certified. Jean Guy Allard was the first to be certified as a Specialist in 1974. 1974 also brought a name change from CCSPE to CAPE (Canadian Association for Pastoral Education/ACEP (Association canadienne pour l'education pastorale). A further name change came 20 years later (1994) when the name became CAPPE (Canadian Association for Pastoral Practice and Education/ACPEP (L'Association canadienne pour la pratique et L'education pastorales) to recognize the growing number of Specialists in the organization. In 2010 the name changed once again to CASC (Canadian Association for Spiritual Care)/ACSS (Association canadienne de soins spirituels) to reflect new realities in the work environment where religious care was replaced with spiritual care. In 1976 reciprocity of certification status with ACPE was approved. Cullene Bryant became the first woman certified as a CPE Teaching Supervisor in 1977, and, in 1981, Ann Evans was certified as a PCE Teaching Supervisor. Elizabeth Kilbourn was elected President of the association in 1981. Its Women's Caucus was created in 1984.

Jan Kraus became the Executive Director (1995), followed in 2001 by Toni Sedfawi. The National A & C Committee was divided into 2 separate committees in 1989 – one looking after accreditation of "centres" and the other the certification of individuals. Under the leadership of Roy Huntley, all teaching centres were required to be accredited. In 1993, Lorraine Nicely and David Wright collaborated to establish a comprehensive Code of Ethics. After adoption, it became part of the educational and peer review process. Every certified member must take an ethics program that must be renewed every five years as part of the peer review process.

A major overhaul of the Certification process took place between 2001 and 2002 and focused on integrating candidates' documentation work with the interview process. Gale Macauley-Newcombe designed the first matrix assessment tool for interfacing required papers with competencies. Becky Vink continued this effort (2011) ultimately leading to the formulation of a set of Competencies for Spiritual Care and Counseling Specialist.

In 2004 CAPPE/ACPEP joined with five other spiritual care organizations to affirm Common Standards. This shared affirmation led to the establishment of The Spiritual Care Collaborative (SCC) in 2007 with AAPC, ACPE, CAPPE/ACPEP, NACC and NAJC as members. In 2015 CASC/ACSS celebrated its golden anniversary in Hamilton, Ontario.[14]

Whereas the context (place) of ministry differs from the other groups highlighted in this volume, the qualities and duties of the next five groups are similar and thus merit inclusion in this updated history of chaplaincy.

Military Chaplains

There is no singular certifying association for military chaplains. Each branch of service has its own requirements that are similar to each other. For example, to become an army chaplain, one must be a U.S. citizen (although for the reserves one can be a permanent resident) and enlist in the Army Chaplain Corps full time. The army chaplain must pass national security clearance and a physical exam, and have two years professional experience as a chaplain. This requirement does not apply to reserves. Applicants must be at least 21 years old and younger than 42 (45 for reserves). Chaplains are required to hold an undergraduate degree as well as a graduate degree in theological studies. They are also expected to present a faith group endorsement stating their clergy status and qualified to act as army chaplains including being sensitive to religious pluralism (http:/work.chron.com/requirements-become-army-chaplain-14316.html). The Navy requires its chaplains to attend Officer Development School and to take a seven-week course at the Naval Chaplain School in South Carolina.

---

[14] For this history the following 3 websites were consulted: http://www.spiritualcare.ca/index.asp http://www.spiritualca re.ca/page.asp?ID=157 and http://www.spiritualcare.ca/researchdetails.asp?ID=138; as well as *CASC/ACSS Policy and Procedure Manual*, chapter 2, section I B. Education Streams and E. Certification, June 2013). Mostly this section was written and approved by Douglas Kellough, Margaret Clark, Douglas Wilson and Marc Doucet (CASC/ACSS) with some editing by me.

There is a Military Chaplains Association of the USA (MCA). This association is for military chaplains who have served in a military branch as a chaplain and who wish to continue their ministry by providing pastoral care to military personnel and their families.

The National Institute of Business and Industrial Chaplains (NIBIC)

According to its website (http://www.nibic.com/703033), a NIBIC chaplain is: an ordained minister, endorsed by their denomination, and able to provide pastoral care and counseling. Chaplains see their work as representing God's care for all; they are colleagues to, not substitutes for, local clergy.

Specifically, Business-Industrial Chaplains (same website) are trained, ordained ministers who provide interdenominational/ecumenical ministry to those in business and industry. They do not compete with community services and are preventative and active in problem-solving within business and industry.

A history of Workplace Chaplaincy provided by Rev. Dr. Diana C. Dale, Executive Director of NIBIC,[15] indicated that workplace ministry has existed in the U.S. since colonial times. In the 1700s and 1800s company logs indicate that a number of companies had chaplaincy services. Modern industrial chaplaincy is thought to have begun in 1931 with the industrialist R.G. LeTourneau who started "shop meetings," counseling and worship services for the Hoover Dam field crews. He continued these practices at his manufacturing plants in Illinois, Georgia and Mississippi. After WWII, workplace chaplaincy focused on the needs of workers returning to the workplace and included employee counseling programs. In the 1970s and 1980s the number and types of workplace ministries expanded to include chaplaincy/employee counseling programs and referrals to outside agencies and associations. The 1980s also saw a broadening of workplace ministry to include working for

---

[15] The unpublished history is entitled "Workplace Chaplaincy in the United States-History and Principles" by The Rev. Diana C. Dale, D.Min., Ph.D., LMFT, and was provided to me as a resource for this book. Originally written in 1992 and most recently revised in 2011.

structural change in workplaces. In the 1990s companies outsourced employee services including counseling resulting in many in-house chaplains being retired and laid off. The last 30 years has seen the development of external chaplaincy providers and the development of chaplaincy provider and mentoring centers. One such center is the Worklife Institute, founded in 1988 in Houston Texas; this location currently serves as the NIBIC'S home.

Workplace chaplains are often called by other titles such as corporate chaplain, pastoral counselor, human resources advisor, and employee counselor, to name a few. They cross-train and provide services with EAP programs, Human Resources, and other programs.

To become a Clinical Member of NIBIC one must have a Bachelor's degree, theological education, ordination or commissioning by a faith group, and four units of CPE. To become a certified chaplain in this association, one must have been a Clinical Member for at least one year and then demonstrate leadership, advanced competence and professional excellence.

American Correctional Chaplains Association (ACCA)

According to the ACCA website (http://www.correctionalchaplains.org/what_is_the_acca.htm), correctional chaplains are a lot like military and hospital chaplains who "provide pastoral care to those who are disconnected from the general community by certain circumstances – in this case those who are imprisoned." Correctional chaplains provide pastoral counseling and marital counseling. They are responsible for liturgical duties, implementing religious program policy, and religious volunteer recruitment, training and coordination. Some correctional facilities have a staff of volunteer chaplains of varying faiths to best serve the needs of those imprisoned. Each correctional facility and/or each faith group decides on the qualifications of their staff chaplains – for instance whether or not they must be ordained.

Roslyn A. Karaban, Ph.D.

International Police and Fire Chaplains Association (IPFCA)

Many cities have chaplains for their police and fire departments. In most cases these are ordained clergy who volunteer their services. There are certifying organizations, such as IPFCA, that provide training for First Responder Chaplains (Police, Fire and Homeland security) as well as other types of chaplaincy. To become a member of IPFCA one must be a Christian Layman (sic), a Minister, or Ordained Minister for at least 3 years (www.IPFCA.org) and feel a calling to this particular type of ministry (http://ipfca.org/membership). IPFCA has chapters across the US as well as in South Africa and India, and is a Christian association requiring that an applicant have sufficient Bible and theological education before beginning training (http://ipfca.org/about). Even after training and certification, IPFCA chaplains are mostly not paid for their chaplaincy work.

Muslim Chaplains Association

More recently, a Muslims Chaplains Association formed (2006) spearheaded by chaplaincy student Bilal Ansari at Hartford Seminary. It quickly grew to 100 members (http://www.muslimchaplains.org/about-us/history). Why a separate Muslim association? An answer may be similar to a separate Jewish and Catholic association. "Islam is the fastest growing major religion among American military personnel" with 4000-10,000 Muslims serving in the U.S. Armed Forces. There were only ten Muslim chaplains in the military in 2001 (http://www.muslimchaplains.org/about-us/faq).[16] More will be said about Muslim and other non-Christian Chaplains in Chapter Four.

---

[16] The estimates of 4000 and 10,000 come from 2 different sources; the former from the military, the latter from Muslim organizations (http://www.muslimchaplains.org/about-us/faq)

Common Core of CPE

The Joint Spiritual Care Summit that took place in Orlando, Florida in 2010 brought together six organizations: NACC, ACPE, NAJC, APC, AAPC and CAPPE. The numerical breakdown of those in attendance was: NAJC- 78, CAPPE – 111, AAPC – 156, NACC - 295, ACPE – 321, and APC – 503 (Email from Sharon Sheflett, AAPC office, August 20, 2013). These numbers are in direct proportion to the association's membership size.

No matter the professional chaplaincy association, the common factor shared by all these organizations is the base of Clinical Pastoral Education. As the field of chaplaincy has grown and become a professional vocation over time, more emphasis is placed on training certification and the completion of four units of CPE. In this context, a question arises for aspiring chaplains, why become certified in one group and not another?

The above history of some of the differences hints at why separate organizations exist. One size does not fit all, and particular religious groups (for instance, Catholics, Jews, and Muslims) still regard the need to have more of a Catholic, Jewish, or Muslim identity in addition to common clinical education. Why choose certification in APC instead of NACC or NAJC or ACPE or CPSP? For three of the final four groups discussed - military chaplains, business chaplains, and correctional chaplains - the place of one's ministry may be the prevalent factor. However, in addition to ACCA, for instance, there is also the ACCCA, the American Catholic Correctional Chaplains Association and as a Catholic Chaplain I may choose this association over ACCA. Therefore, for all the groups mentioned, why someone chooses one group over another is outside the purview of this book.

Chapter Two

Snapshots of Chaplains

Descriptions of Chaplains

This chapter will draw from journal articles published after 1992, as well as statistics provided by the major chaplaincy organizations, to describe the demographics and backgrounds of contemporary chaplains. These descriptions will include religious affiliation, gender, and age, as well as qualities and characteristics.

In the 1998, John Gleason wrote a guest editorial for The Journal of Pastoral Care that compared the old CPE paradigm, particularly in relation to supervisors (pre-1998), with the new (post-1998) (Gleason, 1998, pp.3-4).

Characteristics of Pre-1998 Supervisors

Emphasis on:

Masculinity
Heterosexuality
Protestant
European-American
Ordained
Teaching through confrontation
Learning through mentors

Deep loyalty to spirit of CPE
Hubris (too much pride)
Empathy to suffering individuals
Spontaneity, informality, advocacy for sexual liberation
Psychoanalytic orientation for individual supervision; humanistic for group

Characteristics of Post-1998 Supervisors

Emphasis on:

Parity of femininity with masculinity
Parity of heterosexuality with homosexuality
Multi faith
Parity of race and culture
Mix of clergy and laity
Teaching through confrontation and support
Peer learning
Mixture of old spirit with new
Humility
Empathy extended to societal structures, including disenfranchised women and gays in ministry
Hospitality and egalitarianism
Integration of psychoanalytic and humanistic of psychoanalytic and humanistic
Supervision for individual and group

In short, Gleason argued that changes in relations between men and women, influenced particularly by The Feminist Movement, had a great impact on CPE that created a new model with "increasing number of supervisors, highly developed standards, [and] more formal structures…" (p. 4). These changes continue today.

An article appeared around this same time in The Journal of Pastoral Care by R. Wayne Willis (1999). Willis suggested that the traditional description of the clergyperson as pastor, priest and prophet, can also be used to describe the hospital chaplain (p. 391). However, according to Willis, the term chaplain is not really a helpful term because it basically means a person associated with the chapel. Willis suggests a number of updated metaphors to describe chaplains: Sitter – someone who is present, being with; Scatologist – the garbage collector, the soul cleanser; Seedpicker – one who picks up seeds here and there; Stargazer – one who is concerned with awe and mystery, the beyond, ultimate concerns; The Sistership – someone who represents the rescue ship, the lifeline; Storymeister – the lover and listener of stories; and Spy – the one willing to participate in clandestine activity; God's spy (pp. 392-394).

Another description of the chaplain and of CPE was published around the turn of the century in The Journal of Pastoral Care & Counseling. In this article, part of a guest editorial, John R. DeVelder and Raymond J. Lawrence, described a shift in CPE and thus the chaplain from 1990 to 2003. This shift entailed a new vision that returns to theology, "revivifies" (rejuvenates) personal authority, is part of a more communal political system and sees clinical training as personal transformation rather than skill development (pp.1-2).

Larry VandeCreek and Laurel Burton (Journal of Pastoral Care, Spring 2001, vol. 55, no. 1, pp. 81-97) note that professional chaplains are educators, mediators, reconcilers, contact people, and part of teams (pp. 86-88).

Roslyn A. Karaban, Ph.D.

Statistics from Major Organizations

In part, defining who a chaplain is today depends on the major chaplaincy organization one looks at as well as where the chaplaincy is conducted. As noted in chapter one, the focus for this continuing history is on hospital chaplains. [17]

Association of Clinical Pastoral Education (ACPE)

Karen McCray, former Database Administrator and Membership Coordinator of ACPE, provided the following membership statistics in an August 26, 2013 personal communication:[18]:

Of the 1445 Members in the database across all categories, there were 566 females and 846 males and 33 "not defined."

These numbers are a bit misleading, however, since 246 males were either retired active or inactive and 50 females were retired. The number of female members appears to be on an increase.

Breakdown by Gender

	Females	Males	Not defined	Total
	566	846	33	1445
Retired Active & Retired Inactive	50	246	-	296

---

[17] In the fall of 2012 I was asked to address the NY state meeting of Roman Catholic Prison and Jail Chaplains. Of the approximately 100 chaplains present about 95 were male, primarily ordained deacons or priests; about 92 (of the 95 males) were also Caucasian. Of the 5 or 6 women present, most were women religious; one was the wife of a deacon and one was a RC laywoman with the M.Div. degree.

[18] Whereas these statistics will change a bit by the time this book is published (true for each organization) the statistics given here are meant to be more of a snapshot and to give a picture of who is the chaplain of today. Note also that the number of 1445 for gender does not exactly match the number of 1447 for Religious Affiliation and may be accounted for by members not always choosing to check every box.

ACPE does not compile information about membership race. Additionally, the organization does not keep track of age or age range of its membership. ACPE did provide a breakdown by denomination and religion.

Breakdown by Religious Affiliation - includes all levels of membership

Of the 1447 Members who identified a religious affiliation, the overwhelming majority (1127) in 2013 are Protestant Christians – 1127. Roman Catholics come in second (166), and Jews follow (39), then Buddhists (12). The smallest group was Muslim (2). These categories include all levels of membership. ACPE does not keep a computerized record of how many members are lay or ordained, but it is safe to conclude, that, at least among the Protestant Christians and Jews, the majority are still ordained.

National Association of Catholic Chaplains (NACC)

In a personal communication of May 19, 2015, David Lichter, Executive Director of NACC, provided the following statistics:

	Female	Male	Totals
Certified Members	1084	529	1613
Dually Certified through NACC and ACPE	24	16	40
Laypeople	611	206	817
Religious/Ordained	473	323 (272 priests, 9 brothers, 42 deacons)	796

Clearly, the majority of certified chaplains are female and increasingly they are laity (total 817 lay vs. 796 women religious and the ordained). According to Philip Paradowski, in an August 26, 2013 personal communication, all certified members are Roman

Catholic. NACC tracks age and was able to provide the following statistics: average age of certified chaplain: 64; average age of student: 63 (October 9, 2013 personal communication).

Updated statistics provided by David Lichter in a personal communication of May 19, 2015:

Total membership of 2274 reflects the following:

laywomen	38.9%
women religious	24.4%
priests	17.1%
laymen	15.2%
permanent deacons	3.4%
religious brothers	.07%

65.0% of these members are certified

Another statistic from 2015 is that of the 132 new members, 58 (44%) are laywomen and 20 (8%) are laymen, accounting for more than half of the new membership.

National Association of Jewish Chaplains (NAJC)/Association of Jewish Chaplains (NESHAMA)

In an October 9, 2013 personal communication, Cecille Asekoff, Executive Director of NAJC, broke down Membership in the following way: Total of 583 members – all levels of affiliation

Type	Male	Female	Total
Certified Member	63	50	113
Regular Member	88	86	174
Retired Member	47	9	56
Students	20	42	62
Military	5	2	7

Supporters	64	59	123
Major and Nonprofit Supporters	agencies and organizations		
Total			583

She clarified that all members are Jewish with one non-Jewish supporter. Not all members are Rabbis. "The non clergy (rabbinic) segment of our membership is a fast growing segment. More and more people are choosing chaplaincy as a career. At the moment, we have 160 people who are not Rabbis or Cantors." (C. Asekoff, personal communication, October 9, 2013). NAJC does not track the ages of members, but she was able to say that the average age is 50-60 with newer applicants in their mid- 20's to mid-30's.

Association of Professional Chaplains (APC)

The APC office provided the following statistics: (March 26, 2015)

Breakdown by Religious Affiliation

Roman Catholic	161
Jewish	44
Unitarian Universalist	49
Sikh	1
Sufi	1
Buddhist	15
Christian	4416

Total	4687

Breakdown by Gender

	Male	Female	Not Specified	Total
Affiliate	493	515	84	1092
Associate Certified Chaplain	35	21		56
Board Certified Chaplain	1344	1095	28	2467
Corporate Affiliate	2	1		3
Corporate Associate Certified	1	1		2
Corporate Board Certified	15	13	1	29
Life Affiliate 80+	4	2		6
Life Institutional Member – AC	1			1
Life Institutional Member – BCC	10	1		11
Life Professional Member – AC	6	5		11
Life Retired Associate Certified 80+	15	3		18
Life Retired Board Certified 80+	97	13	1	111
Life Retired Member – AC	3	1		4
Life Retired Member – BCC	34	10	1	45
Provisional Associate Certified Chaplain	1	2	1	4
Provisional Board Certified Chaplain	26	37		63
Retired Affiliate		1		1
Retired Associate Certified Chaplain	7	10		17
Retired Board Certified Chaplain	286	215	2	503
Student	92	128	23	243
Grand Total	2472	2074	141	4687

With regard to how many of the Board Certified Chaplains are ordained, Diane Gerard stated: "All Board, Certified and Provisional Certified members must be ordained or commissioned to function in a ministry of pastoral care. We do not keep track who was ordained or who was commissioned." (D. Gerard, personal communication, September 27, 2013).

For APC age is an optional field for members and is not tracked (D. Gerard, personal communication, October 8, 2013).

The College of Pastoral Supervision and Psychotherapy (CPSP)

The following numbers came from the Directory available online and was accessed and tabulated by me on December 5, 2014. The numbers are approximations. It was not always possible to tell gender by name, and some names had no title associated with them.

CPSP

	Male	Female	Total
Diplomates in Pastoral Supervision	58	16	74
Clinical Chaplains	210	148	358
Associate Clinical Chaplains (lay chaplains, do not have levels of theological education required of clergy)	28	44	72
Total	296	352	648

The Canadian Association for Spiritual Care (CASC)/Association canadienne de soins spirituels (ACSS)

The following statistics were available from Toni Sedfawi, Executive Director of CASC/ACSS in a November 20, 2013 email:

CASC/ACSS

Associate Members	528
Certified Members	295
Member Emeritus	87
Student Members	187
Education Centers	39

Information regarding age, religious affiliation, gender, etc. was not available.

Chaplains: Summary

In summarizing the chaplain of today, some characteristics are not noted or obvious in the previous statistics. For instance, very important aspects of being a professional chaplain today are the qualities, values, and skills necessary to being a chaplain. The qualities needed to be a hospice chaplain include compassion, openness, sensitivity, courage and hope and the skills entail empathy, knowledge, and assertiveness (Karaban, 2006, 14-16). Some of these qualities could readily describe the hospital chaplain of today, but a better description of qualities and competencies comes from the 2010 ACPE[19] Standards (Standard 101, p. 2) stating that a member: (Standard 101, p. 2) affirms and respects the dignity of each person, does not discriminate, respects those served or supervised and does not emotionally or sexually exploit. A member approaches religious beliefs of all with respect and avoids imposing own theology, respects confidentiality and follows research guidelines.[20]

Standard 311 lists the Outcomes expected at the conclusion of CPE Level I students in the areas of pastoral formation, pastoral competence and pastoral reflection; Standard 312 lists the Outcomes expected at the conclusion of CPE Level II students in these same areas; and Standards 314-319 list the Outcomes expected of Supervisors in the areas of competence as a pastoral supervisor, competence in the theories of supervision, competence in the practice of CPE and supervision, competence in CPE program design and implementation, and competence in pastoral education (Standards, pp. 14-18).

---

[19] Revised Standards from 2016 can be found in the citation references.
[20] Standards 102, 103, 104 and 105 may also be referenced here (pp. 3-4).

The Standards can be accessed online at: http://www.acpe.edu/NewPDF/2010%20Manuals/2010%20Standards.pdf.

Professional chaplains today are just as likely to be female as male, still predominantly Protestant – with Roman Catholics, Jews and Muslims on the increase. They are still more likely to be ordained (except for Roman Catholics and faith groups that do not ordain women.) Chaplains today are more likely to be second-career people, in their 40's, 50's and above (note NACC statistics), seeing chaplaincy as their call, their ministry, or their charge. They are educated and professional. They share a common core of CPE as a component of their education. They are paid for their chaplaincy work. To quote from the website of the Muslim Chaplains Association:

> A chaplain is a professional who offers spiritual advice and care in a specific institutional context, such as a military unit or college campus, hospital or prison. Although chaplains often provide religious services for members of their own faith communities, the main role of a chaplain is to facilitate or accommodate the religious needs of all individuals in the institution in which he or she is working.
>
> Chaplains often serve as experts on ethics to their colleagues and employers, providing insight to such diverse issues as organ transplantation, just-warfare, and public policy. Professional chaplains do not displace religious leaders, but fill the special requirements involved in intense institutional environments.
>
> Thus, a Muslim chaplain is not necessarily an "Imam," although an Imam may work as a chaplain. There is a need for both male and female Muslim chaplains. For example, female Muslim students on college campuses or hospitalized Muslim women may feel more

comfortable with a Muslim woman chaplain. (http://www.muslimchaplains.org/about-us/faq)

NACC offers a comparison between the roles of a chaplain prior to 2000 and post-2000 titled "Evolution of the Chaplain's Role" (www.nacc.org/docs/resources/NACC-Evolution520of%20) adding some of the following updates: The chaplain post-2000 is part of an interdisciplinary team where s/he is seen as the spiritual care expert/professional. S/he is an educator/coach/mentor, a partner and facilitator. The chaplain is a layperson, woman religious, priest, deacon or ordained minister who is able to triage, chart and use technology.

According to the Common Standards for Professional Chaplaincy document adopted by APC, AAPC, ACPE, NACC, NAJC and CASC in 2004, professional chaplains must have completed an undergraduate degree from an accredited school, a graduate-level theological degree from an accredited school, and have completed 4 units of CPE accredited by ACPE, USCCB, or CAPPE/ACPEP. (See Index for copy of Common Standards.)

The role of the chaplain today continues to evolve and expand. The next chapter will focus on where and how chaplaincy is done.

CHAPTER THREE

Where and How

Where is CPE Offered Today?

Institutions

According to the ACPE website (http://acpe.edu/), CPE is offered "in hospitals and health care including university, children's, and veterans' facilities; in hospices; in psychiatric and community care facilities; in workplace settings; in geriatric and rehabilitation centers; and in congregational and parish-based settings." Again, according to their website http://www.acpe.edu/DirectoriesDortedE.html), current sites where CPE is conducted include the following locations:

Institutions Accredited by ACPE to Offer CPE

General Hospitals	120
Multi-institutional centers (primarily health care and medical centers)	70
Children's hospitals	6
Psychiatric hospitals	7
Veterans hospitals	22
Counseling centers	2
Community mental health centers	0

Adult correctional centers	0
Juvenile correctional centers	1
Parish-based centers	4
Developmentally disabled/mental health centers	2
Retirement/geriatric facilities	7
Rehabilitation centers	0
Military centers	7
Alcohol and drug addiction centers	0
Hospice sites	8
Pastoral care agency	1
Campus ministry settings	0
Trauma I centers	25
Theological seminaries	2
Theological seminaries whose sites are all medical centers, hospitals and health care systems	43

Including all hospitals and medical centers, in this ACPE report, the vast majority, 293, account for CPE training. All other sites total only 34. Owing to the high prevalence of CPE training in hospital settings I have focused on CPE and chaplaincy primarily in this arena.

Countries

ACPE has no fully accredited CPE programs outside of the United States and Canada. This feature should not suggest that professional chaplaincy is lacking or not developing elsewhere. This chapter, and the next, will explore some of the programs taking place on the international scene.

According to the ACPE website (http://acpe.edu/Directories InternationalAffiliates.html) there are eight International Affiliate Members Organizations/Entities which are:

- Africa University in Zimbabwe
- Alice Ho Miu Ling Nethersole Hospital, the Association of Hong Kong Hospital Christian Chaplaincy Ministry and Hong Kong Baptist Hospital – all in Hong Kong
- Cameroon Baptist Convention Health Board – in Cameroon
- Crisis Assessment and Recovery (CARE) Center, Presbyterian Church of East Africa, and Servants of the Sick – Training Centre for Healthcare Ministry – all in Kenya

According to Hall (1992, p. 191), one of the two most dramatic new directions in ACPE in the 1980's and 1990's was the international development identified in the brief history that follows.

According to Minutes of the ACPE Board of Representatives, interest in developing centers in other countries began in the mid-1990's. In 1996 a new membership category was created: Foreign Affiliate Center. This category was designed for emerging CPE centers in foreign countries desiring a non-accredited filial relationship with ACPE. Also, around this time ACPE became a founding member of NIC (National Interfaith Coalition for Spiritual Care and Counseling). The ACPE President appointed a representative to NIC's Board of Directors. In 1997, Hong Kong Hospital Christian Chaplaincy Ministry, Ktd, was accepted as the first International Affiliate Organization of ACPE, followed by Alice Ho Miu Nethersole Hospital in Hong Kong.

By 2001 a flurry of activity was reported in the Minutes of the Board of Representatives that included the following:

- Appointing a task force to address recommendations on international relations
- Creating a category of membership for those who obtain ACPE Associate Supervisor and return to their home country
- Initiating an exchange program with one or more CPE programs in other countries for domestic students to enroll in CPE abroad and receive ACPE credit

- Seeking funding for ACPE supervisors to conduct CPE in other countries
- Defining ACPE's policy on assisting with the startup of CPE programs in other countries

In the fall of 2007, Cameroon Baptist Convention Health Board was accepted as an International Affiliate and in 2007 and 2008, two U.S. Supervisors provided CPE at Africa University in Zimbabwe. In 2009, a Norwegian CPE program was started with students training in the US. In 2010 the Association of Hong Kong Hospital Chaplaincy Ministry, Ltd. was accepted to be a corporate member of the Oversea Consultant Network. Before moving on to the increasing international development of chaplaincy and pastoral/spiritual care in additional countries, it is important to note the broader context in which this outreach and these international ties occurred.

CPSP

Of the 86 training centers accredited by CPSP, two are inactive, and more than half are in hospitals, medical centers, and hospice facilities. Twenty of the programs are outside of the United States:

Bukal Life Care and Counseling, Inc.	Baguio City
Codrington College	Barbados
The Hospital for Sick Children	Canada
Clinical Pastoral Centre of Toronto	Canada
Anglican Diocese of Cape Coast	Central Region, Ghana, West Africa
Bethel Bible Seminary	Hong Kong
Hong Kong Baptist Hospital	Hong Kong
Hong Kong Sheng Kung Hui (Anglican Church)	Hong Kong
Ufficio di Pastorale Clinica	Italy

MI-CPE, The Anglican Diocese of West Malaysia	Malaysia
Mayaguez CPE Center	Mayaguez, Puerto Rico
Philippine Children's Medical Center	Metro Manila
Philippine Baptist Theological Seminary	Philippines
Philippine Advocates for Resilient Communities, Inc. (PARC)	Philippines
Hospital San Francisco	Puerto Rico
St. Andrew's Community Hospital	Singapore
St. Vincent's Hospital	South Korea
Kilimanjaro Christian Medical Center	Tanzania
Diocese of Koforidua	West Africa
St. Nicholas Seminary	West Africa

ACPE Context

As noted previously, until the 1970's, CPE and, thus, ACPE, were primarily composed of white, male, Protestant pastors. Women met at the national meeting of ACPE for the first time in 1974. In 1980 there were very few people of color in CPE, and George Polk began a task force to investigate this limitation. ACPE determined to rectify this reality, and by the 1990's the Racial/Ethnic Minority Task Force (REM) was up and running. Additionally, a Gay-Lesbian Network was formed. Relationships with NACC and NAJC were expanded. In the fall of 2007, a Leadership In-Service on Multi-Cultural Diversity was conducted. The following year, the theme for the National Conference was "Courageous Conversations: Division, Diversity and Dialogue". Four years later, this theme was a 25th Anniversary Invitational in community with the REM.

In 2010 ACPE identified a number of Strategic Issues to be addressed. Strategic Issue #2 was: "To embrace a multi-cultural, multi-faith identity as an organization and as educators." The above references represent a few of the shifts emerging in ACPE and chaplaincy in general, all designed to become more inclusive and multicultural. This expansive process continues today.

Broader Context

Internationally, significant growth in the broad field of pastoral/spiritual care and counseling took place in the last decade of the 20th century. In 1990 and 1991, the Journal of Supervision and Training in Ministry, volumes 12 and 13, devoted sections to International Supervision, Education, Ministry and CPE in Samoa, Southern Africa, Africa, Indonesia, Japan, New Zealand, Korea, Taiwan and Holland.

At the beginning of the 21st century, Dr. Emmanuel Lartey, originally from Ghana, wrote:

> Pastoral care is dependent upon the cultures, reigning philosophies, and psychologies of the periods in which it is practiced. Forms of pastoral care and counseling practiced in Western societies in the twentieth century and now the twenty-first century reflect the dominant social, cultural, theological, and psychological theories of the West. There are real differences between theories and practices of effective pastoral care and counseling in different parts of the globe. (Lartey, 2004, p. 92).

In this context, it is important to consider what was and is happening in non-western and western, (non-North American) cultures. The first international ecumenical council on pastoral care and counseling took place in Edinburgh, Scotland in 1979. More than 400 participants from all the continents attended. Since that time, the International Council of Pastoral Care and Counseling (ICPCC) has held meetings every four years in San Francisco, USA; Melbourne,

Australia; Noordwijerhout, Netherlands; Toronto, Canada; Acra, Ghana; Bangalore, India; Krzyzowa, Poland; Rotorua, New Zealand, and, in San Francisco (2015).

These conferences and the concomitant trends in pastoral care represent a progression from globalization and exporting and importing into cultures "worldview, values, theological anthropology, lifestyle, paradigms, and forms of practice developed in North America and western Europe" (Lartey, 2004 p. 88). According to Lartey, there is at least an internationalization effort that represents an integrative approach to local contexts/cultures "by placing Western theories and practices alongside non-Western, local ones" (p. 89) and moving toward indigenization, utilizing practices and models indigenous to the non-Western culture (p. 90).

Lartey's essay, "Globalization, Internationalization, and Indigenization of Pastoral Care and Counseling," features the pastoral care and counseling activities, models, and organizations in The Philippines, Korea, China, India, Africa, Latin America and Europe. It is a pivotal work to understanding both the limitations, challenges and possibilities for pastoral/spiritual care in the future.

Today

Though it is beyond the scope of this book to provide the details of all the different groups that have emerged around the world and their impact on pastoral/spiritual care, counseling and chaplaincy in the U.S., it is important to identify some of these shifts and trends. This chapter offers limited comment on the impact that other cultures and religious traditions have had on CPE chaplaincy training in the U.S.[21] It remains important to consider how the presence of students from other countries and other cultures and other religious traditions has affected the US CPE culture. Similarly, it is important

---

[21] Hopefully, future studies will consider and include the international development of chaplaincy and spiritual care. See Appendix 2 for a partial listing of International programs.

to identify how supervisors who have taught diverse groups and sometimes supervised in other countries have changed and how they are adapting to these expansions.

Many articles appearing in The Journal of Pastoral Care and Counseling from the year 2000 and beyond, and one from Reflective Practice: Formation and Supervision in Ministry (volume 27, 2007) reflect the animated growth and expansion pastoral and spiritual care globally. For example, Soo-Young Kwon and Anthony Duc Le suggest how CPE Supervisors and Students can dialogue to create mutual understanding and help Asian[22] students translate CPE into their own cultural context (2004). The authors point out that they were influenced by a Confucian model of relationships characterized by a two-dimensional view of the person – autonomous and relational, integral and inseparable, as opposed to the western model of CPE that emphasizes a verbalization of relationships, sharing of personal information, and a model of equal relationships that are challenging for Asian students (pp. 203-21). The authors suggest that at the very least, more translation is needed (p. 214).

In 2000, Homer Jernigan published an article entitled, "Clinical Pastoral Education with Students from Other Cultures: The Role of the Supervisor," in The Journal of Pastoral Care. His focus was on providing CPE with students of other cultures based on his experience in Asia, and with Asian students in Boston. He highlighted that ACPE needs to develop "culturally appropriate programs of CPE" around the world (p. 135) that would replace the old model of U.S. CPE Supervisors going to other countries and students from other countries coming to the U.S. to take CPE. He proposed that indigenous supervisors need to be trained. As with Kwon and Duc Le, Jernigan (2004) considered translation to be the key (p. 136) but noted that much can be lost in translation. In this context, dialogue, respect and standing with students on the boundaries between

---

[22] Asian in this article refers to China, Korea, Japan and Vietnam (p.204).

cultures becomes essential (p. 137). He puts forth three tasks for Supervisors to stand with Students on the boundary:

- Develop empirical and empathic understanding of the student's culture
- Use that understanding to look at one's own culture (comparative mirror)
- Clarify differences between CPE as "subculture" and "classical" US theological education (p. 139)

Two books in the field of pastoral/spiritual care, Hall's Head and Heart, and Vision from a Little Known Country: A Boisen Reader (Glenn H. Asquith, Jr., Editor) were translated into Korean (2015).

Model of Indigenization

Jan de Jong's (2007) article, "Toward Indigenous CPE: A Mini-CPE Program at Grey's Hospital, Pietermaritzburg KwaZulu-Natal" published in Reflective Practice in Ministry: Formation and Supervision in Ministry, described how a Mini-CPE Program in KwaZulu-Natal, South Africa attempted to "inculturate (sic) CPE in a South African context" (p. 176). He asked a crucial question at the heart of the possibility of indigenizing CPE:

> How does clinical pastoral education (CPE) – which found its origin in a predominantly male, white, and liberal Protestant North American environment – flourish today in different parts of the world? Although CPE originated in the United States, can it be successfully translated to different cultural contexts (p. 175)?

Supervisors included a Zimbabwean Lutheran pastor, a Zimbabwean Catholic Sister, a Catholic priest from Wisconsin, and the author. The group was comprised of eight students – four from South Africa and one each from Zimbabwe, Namibia, Zambia, and the Philippines. Two critical issues emerged: (1) language and (2) the pervasiveness of HIV/AIDS among the hospital patients. Although the morning devotion took place in numerous African languages, the didactics and seminars were in English, and verbatims and reports were written and shared in English. English was the third language for many of the students. Additionally, more than 70% of the patients in the hospital were HIV infected or had AIDS. Many of the CPE students had personally experienced the death of a loved one to AIDS. This feature had a profound effect on the approach to their chaplaincy work.

De Jong concluded that this program represented an attempt to develop an indigenous CPE program. Language remained an issue throughout, but he thought that through words and listening (palaver), community was established. The concept of Ubuntu was central, a person becomes a person through others; I am because we are was honored; sensitivity to and respect for each student's religion and values was an important guiding principle, as was a sensitivity to a student's psychology. Finally, sensitivity to the student's learning style became both communal and experiential (pp. 182-184).[23]

Being both intrigued and overwhelmed by what is taking place in other countries with the development of indigenous theories, models, and training programs, I concluded that, as a European-American, it would be prudent to leave the tracking of these developments to a non- European-American author and to another book.

---

[23] De Jong also refers to a lecture given by John DeVelder that enumerated "Principles of Indigenous CPE" at the REM Invitational in 2006. These principles are: language, culture, sensitivity to student's religion and values, sensitivity to student's psychology – individual and community, and sensitivity to student's learning style.

How is CPE Taught Today?

Curriculum

Even though latitude exists in the exact formatting of a CPE program and the variety of topics, there are a number of common characteristics to a CPE curriculum (ACPE 2010 Standards):

A unit of CPE is at least 400 hours with at least 100 hours of group and individual education (308.1). A "relational learning environment" is essential (308.5). The instructional plan must include: student goals, a core curriculum, a syllabus, evidence of congruence between program goals and the mission of the institution, and a student program evaluation (308.6). The curriculum must address theoretical foundations of clinical pastoral supervision and a bibliography needs to include: the history of CPE, theology, educational theory, behavioral sciences, multicultural theory, management and administration of educational programs, group theory, supervisory theory and personal and professional ethics (308.9.5).

A typical CPE curriculum would have some or all of the following components: a Learning Contract with learning objective, a weekly reflection paper due every week and verbatims of patient visits. An Interpersonal Relations Seminar (IPR) is held with other CPE students to integrate personal and professional issues in the context of group relationships. Various expert presenters lead didactics. Topics may include clinical ethics, grief and loss, self-care, pediatrics and palliative care. Monthly Rounds with Medical Personnel are another important component. Individual supervision is conducted weekly. Readings are assigned according to the learning objectives by the supervisor and the presenters. Each student needs to prepare and lead a worship service. The supervisor and each student write mid-Term and Final Evaluations. Residents also need to present periodic case studies.

Level I, Level II and Supervisory CPE

Each ACPE accredited center designs its own curriculum (in keeping with the above). ACPE accredits Level I, Level II and Supervisory CPE programs. Level I curriculum outcomes must be met before admission to Level II, and Level I and II outcomes must be completed before admission to Supervisory CPE.

For both Level I and Level II students must achieve specific objectives in Pastoral Formation, Pastoral Competence, Pastoral Reflection (Standards 309, 310, 311 and 312) and for Supervisory CPE students must demonstrate competency: (Standards 314-319) as a pastoral supervisor in the theories of supervision, the practice of individual and group supervision, as well as in CPE program design and education and pastoral education.

As previously noted, both the content and pedagogy CPE are largely influenced and developed in a western, North-American context with some adjustments made for students from other countries and cultures, or when CPE is taught in another country and culture. However, this model is one of globalization (Lartey 2004, p. 88) or importing and exporting North American and Western European worldview, values, and ethics. At the turn of the last century, there were attempts at dialogue between cultures, what Lartey calls internationalization (p.89). He points to the International Council on Pastoral Care and Counseling (ICPCC) and the Society for Intercultural Pastoral Care and Counseling (SIPCC) as doing this (p. 89). He argues that what is needed most, however, is the model of indigenization (p. 90) that is happening most markedly in India (p. 100). The curriculum of CPE is just beginning to move in this direction in North America.

Chapter Four

The Current Scene

The last three chapters describe the history of clinical pastoral education (CPE) and chaplaincy from 1992 to the present. However, 2010-2017 resulted in radical shifts, trends, and changes in chaplaincy that this book only begins to touch upon. This chapter describes chaplaincy currently and projects its evolving context in two different ways by: (1) referring to recent articles and research studies that suggest and point to trends and developments in the discipline and (2) summarizing the results of a survey the author conducted in co-operation with the 7 major chaplaincy organizations.

Recent Scholarship on the Future Directions of Chaplaincy

Chapter three suggests that the curriculum of CPE needs to shift if it is to truly honor the multi-faith and multi-cultural worlds of both the students that take CPE as part of their chaplaincy training and the people to whom they provide care and counseling. Recent articles in The Journal of Pastoral Care & Counseling address a number of curriculum concerns. In 2010, N. Keith Little of Australia, assessed the CPE curriculum in relation to training Christian ministers for pastoral care, and compares the methodology of CPE training with a professional education model. Little names a number of limitations in the present curriculum with suggestions for change. He first defines Christian pastoral care[24] as the responsibility of all church members (p. 1) and notes that in order to provide effective care, "pastoral workers require a deep self-awareness and …professional knowledge, skill and boundaries" (p.1). He argues that historically clergy were seen as professionals. However, since then, they have given over much of their roles to other professions. Little maintains that with the emergence and rise of CPE training programs, some of that concept of professionalism has returned. Little traces the tie of profession/professionalism back to Edward Thornton's history of CPE (p. 2), Professional Education for Ministry, 1970. He then examines CPE through a professional model that focuses on a: (1) knowledge base, (2) service ideal, and (3) public trust and personal autonomy (Bennett & Hokenstad, 1973, p. 1).

Little noted problems with the current CPE educational model beginning with who is admitted into a basic unit. In one group there may be seminary students beginning their education with limited theological knowledge and practical experience in ministry, and theological students with more theological knowledge and practical ministerial experience, and non-theological students with no theological education but with life experience. At the core of this shift is what Little referred to as "a right to a fair experience" (p. 3). He notes that "The challenge is to define what knowledge and how much …is essential before the supervisor can admit a person into a program" (p. 4).

Little concluded by stating, "In many respects CPE fulfills the requirements of practical professional training for pastoral care for clergy and laypeople" (p. 7). However, he enumerated a number of weaknesses that need to be corrected in order to improve the professionalization of CPE programs: "the defining of more precise entry requirements, attending more closely curricula matters, writing

---

[24] Little limits his comments to Christian pastoral care (p.1).

clearer standards and reliable and valid assessment procedures for competence…and linking CPE training more closely with theological colleges" (p. 7).

In March 2012, JPC&C featured an article by Fitchett, Tartaglia, Dodd-McCue, and Murphy that noted how the recently approved Standards of practice included a standard (Standard 12) that acknowledged "the importance of research-literacy for all board-certified chaplains" (p. 2). Fitchett et al randomly selected 26 programs of CPE centers with residency programs, and conducted interviews regarding current practices concerning research in their residency training programs. They found that 62% of the sampled programs reported no research education in their Center (p.4). Only 12% of the programs reported that they have "intentional and substantive research training in their programs" (p.8). Although it is always dangerous to draw conclusions from limited research, this study at least suggests that including research training in CPE curricula has not yet taken hold.

Tartaglia, Fitchett, Dodd-McCue, Murphy, and Derrickson (2013) followed up this research in the next year and identified 11 programs that did offer education in research as part of their residency training, and suggested models and methodologies that other CPE programs could emulate Tartaglia et al concluded:

> CPE programs considering initiating efforts to include research in the curriculum would be served by beginning with realistic aims about the level of research competency to which they can teach. Thoughtful consideration of learning outcomes as well as the methods and resources to meet them would follow as with the development of the remainder of the CPE curriculum. (p. 13)

Kevin Massey wrote in Reflective Practice: Formation and Supervision in Ministry (2014), that "CPE has an important role to play in the earlier formation of persons for ministry. At the same time, it may be ill designed to deliver the techniques, skills and advanced competencies to work in professional chaplaincy." (p. 147) Massey suggested a new kind of CPE residency for the professional chaplain. The remainder of the volume was devoted to responses to his article. The next year Reflective Practice continued addressing CPE training with an article by Alexander Tartaglia (2015) entitled "Reflections on the Development and Future of Chaplaincy Education." Tartaglia suggested a new curricula model for chaplaincy training "that draws upon the ethical assumptions underlying CPE, the historical development of the movement, and the contemporary healthcare environment that is calling for a new environment" (p. 117). Once again, the remainder of the volume was devoted to responses to Tartaglia's proposals.

These brief references to some of the current articles, research projects, suggestions and projections represent just a small cross-section of the explosion of articles currently being written to improve the training programs in CPE-based chaplaincy. Any sequel to this book will likely examine in detail these emerging models and criticisms in light of a multi-cultural and multi-religious world here in North America and beyond.

Broadening the Conversation through Survey

Years ago I served on a curriculum revision committee that spent two years surveying and interviewing former students to determine what they liked about their seminary curriculum and what needed to be changed. The committee analyzed hundreds of responses and the vast majority of respondents indicated that the two most helpful areas of preparation were in Bible and Preaching. This effort took place at an inter-denominational Protestant seminary. The committee noted that if something were to be added to the seminary training, it should be more preparation for the everyday life of a pastor that ranges from hospital visits to fixing furnaces and air conditioners. After much talk and deliberation, the seminary decided to change its curriculum by eliminating requiring core courses like Bible and Preaching and adding two specialized programs that became the signature programs of the seminary. Both programs serve specific needs in the field and in the churches. However, these actions also reflected a case of not listening to those in the field and what they needed and wanted.

This book has been written under guidance. Nonetheless, it still reflects much of my own perspectives and interpretations. Therefore, to expand perspectives included in the book, I contacted chaplaincy organizations and conducted a survey. The initial survey (distributed through Survey Monkey) was sent to a group of local hospital and hospice chaplains to receive feedback on the survey itself. Out of a group of 10 chaplains surveyed, eight responded with helpful suggestions, and the survey was revised. The revised version was sent to the JPCP Board of Managers, and, again, feedback was incorporated. Finally, all seven of the major certifying chaplaincy organizations were invited to participate in the survey (APC, ACPE, NAJC, CPSP, NACC, CASC/ACSS and NIBIC). Each group was asked to submit the email address from every 25th member on their membership list so that I could send the member an email containing the invitation to participate in the study and a survey link. A few of the organizations (ACPE, NACC, NIBIC and CPSP) followed the requested model, and the survey was distributed in that way. NAJC and CASC/ACSS chose to send the survey with their own email and APC allowed it to be put on their Linked-In page. Due to the differing methods, it became hard to achieve an accurate count of exactly how many surveys were distributed. However, after allowing several weeks for the process to be completed, a total of 54 responses were received. Two respondents stated that they did not wish their responses to be published, even anonymously. Therefore, a total of 52 responses will be summarized. Because these responses are a random sampling, no definitive conclusions should be drawn. Nevertheless, they expand the conversation by providing feedback from chaplains in the field.

Of the 52 respondents, 34 were male and 18 were female; 46 respondents identified the US as their home; 4 indicated Canada, (1 indicated a US residency with dual citizenship with Canada), and 1 checked Namibia.

The age breakdown is as follows:

Age	Count
25-30	2
31-35	3
36-40	0
41-45	1
46-50	8
51-55	10
56-60	7
61-65	12
66-70	5
71-75	1
76-80	2
Unidentified	1

When asked to identify their organization, a variety of responses were indicated:

AAPC: 2
AP: 2
ACPE: 1
ASC/ACSS: 1
CPSP: 1
NACC: 3
NAJC, APC: 1

NIB: 1
Aurora Health Care
Bon Secours Hampton Roads
Carolinas Healthcare System
Carondelet Health Network
Catholic Church
Centered Life
CHRISTUS Health
CHRISTUS St, Frances Cabrini Hospital, Alexandria, LA
Denver Health Medical Center
Faith based healthcare
Generations Hospice
Hospice & hospital
IU Health
Kaiser
Louisiana State Police
Maryknoll
Masonicare Partners Hospice
Mercy Health
Mount Sinai Hospital
Muslim Spiritual Care Services
National Lutheran Communities and Services
Ontario Public Service
Penn Highlands Healthcare DuBois
Presence Health
Robert Wood Johnson University Hospital Hamilton
Self-Employed
Seton Heallth Care
St. Boniface Hospital
State of Maryland Division of Corrections and Western Maryland Health System
Sutter Health
ThedaCare

Unity Point Health
UVA Health System
VA
Vermeer Corporation
Veterans Health Care of the Ozarks
Visiting Nurse Hospice
Visiting Nurse Service of Rochester
Without position

When asked specifically which spiritual/pastoral groups they belong to (with a specific list given and the opportunity to add), the following responses were received:

CASC/ACSS	3
AAPC	3
SPT	1
ACPE	12
AAR	0
NACC	10
NAJC	1
APC	27
CPSP	3
NIBIC	3
None	3
Other (please specify) or use for additional information	10

-Global Network on Spirituality and Health (GNSAH) based at George Washington University
-Muslim Chaplains Association
-Clinical member with ACPE, Board Certified Chaplain with APC, and also a Certified Clinical

Correctional Chaplain with ACCA-NAVAC - The National Association of Veterans Affairs Chaplains
-Endorsed by the United Methodist Endorsing Agency
-AACCC
-United Methodist Chaplains

The largest number of respondents came from APC. This may be for a number of reasons: they are the group with the largest membership and the method they chose to advertise the survey was Linked In. This method evoked more responses than personal invitations from the President of the organization, or an email invitation from the author.

As far as Denomination/Faith group was concerned, there was quite a variety:

Adventist	1
AME	1
Baptist	1
Assemblies of God	1
RC	1
Christian	5
Christian Church (Disciples of Christ)	1
Conservative Congregational Christian Conference	1
Evangelical Churches	3
Interfaith	1
Jewish	1
Latter-day Saint	1
Lutheran	2
Muslim	1
Nazarene	1
Non-denominational	2

Prefer not to respond	1
Presbyterian	2
Quaker	1
UCC	1
United Methodist	5

Of these, 32 are ordained, 10 are lay, 3 are religious, 1 is a recorded minister and 6 skipped the question.

Years worked in the field are as follows:

1-5	15
6-10	5
11-15	7
16-20	12
21-25	3
26-30	5
31-35	2
36-40	5

When asked where they currently work, and where chaplains in their organization work, the responses were:

Self	
Hospital	36
Hospice	10
Academic Setting	4
Military	1
Jail	1
Prison	3
Church	4
Synagogue	0

Temple	0
Mosque	1
Industry	1
Health Care	14
Private Practice	3
Counseling Center	1
Retired	5
Other	7

-Currently without a position
-Red Cross Disaster Response
-Retirement community
-LTC, ADC, SLA/CLF
-CPE Training Centre
-"Parish military"
-Former Psychiatric Hospital Spiritual Care Provider

Their organization:

Hospital	42
Hospice	31
Military	7
Academic setting	7
Jail	10
Prison	11
Business	7
Other	11

-Currently without a position
-Community based care
-Also am called on from time to time to consult prison chaplain visitations for inmates incarcerated at our county detention center. I am presently visiting

an 18 year old weekly who has no family and virtually no friends.
-Retirement communities and long-term care.
-Law Enforcement
-"LTC - Long Term Care; Rehab; Adult Day Centers; Supportive Living and Community Arrangement programs"
-CPE Chaplain Educators
-"senior residence, psychiatric institution, parish"
-Private practice
"Skilled Nursing Facilities, Comfort Care Homes"

As far as education is concerned, the Question (#8) asked was whether they received a degree as part of chaplaincy training, and if so, what type of degree

Bachelors	8
Masters	36
Doctorate	5
Advanced degree	3
Certificate	8
Other	8

-Graduate Certificate of Islamic Chaplaincy
-Two Master degrees, M.Ed. in counseling, and M.Div. in Pastoral Leadership
-4 units CPE
-N/A
-I got a Master's later
-I achieved certification as an Associate Clinical Chaplain
Plus course work for a M.A. in Religious Studies
-Certification

The type of training:

Formal theological training	41
Formal psychological training	9
CPE training	45
Other	7

    -Continuing Education
    -Bioethics
    -Fellowship in Clinical Ethics
    -U.S. Navy Chaplain School
    -Masters in Counselling Psychology later
    -on the job training
    -field education, internships

What was missing in your training?

More relational training	5
More economics of health care training	13
More theological training	15
More clinical training	4
More CPE training	4
Nothing missing	18
Other	6

    -How to survive as a chaplain in today's healthcare world. How to keep one's position.
    -creating presence in the clinical setting
    -Leadership/organizational culture training
    -I gained more training on my own (and still studying)
    -more about spirituality
    -more training in rituals, beliefs, and practices from different faiths

What is your department called?

Chaplaincy	15
Pastoral Care	14
Spiritual Care	24
Other	9

-Chaplaincy Care
-Spiritual Health
-Organizationally often "Spiritual Care" is used.
-Palliative Care Chaplain
-Religious Services
-Training Centre
-ACPE
-We do not have a department as such, just called Hospice chaplains.
-Pastoral & Spiritual Care

Summary of Findings

The majority of respondents fell in the age group of 46-65 – more than 70%; this is in keeping with the reports from the 7 organizations that indicate that most of their chaplains fall into this age group. Although all of the 7 major organizations were represented, the highest number of responses (49) came from ACPE, NACC and APC. As previously noted, this may have been due to the method used to solicit responses. The denomination/faith group response came primarily from Christian denominations. An anomaly here is that although 10 responses were from NACC members, only 1 response indicated the respondent was Roman Catholic. More than half the respondents (67%) indicated they were ordained or Religious, but 6 respondents skipped this question. Years worked in the field was split almost equally – 1-10 years: 20; 11-20 years:19 and 21-40 years: 15. Most indicated that they were employed in either hospital or hospital settings, as were chaplains in their professional organization. More than 75% had completed formal theological training and held a masters or doctoral degree. More than 85% had taken CPE as part of their training. These results are in keeping with the requirements for membership/certification in the 7 major organizations. The one category that may indicate shifts that are occurring in the field is in the category of what the department is currently called: Close to 30% call their department some form of pastoral; about 35% use the word chaplaincy in their department name; more than 50% use the word spiritual in the title of their department. This seems to be in keeping with a more inclusive inter-faith perspective.

Although no definitive conclusions can be drawn from this limited study, hopefully these results contribute to broadening the conversation by including other voices from the field.

Chapter Five

Reflections

Personal Reflection

I cannot believe I started writing this book over five years ago. During that brief time new chaplaincy organizations have arisen. One such is the Center for Spiritual Care and Pastoral Formation (CSCPF). Additionally, a new online service called ChaplainsOnHand arose providing the ability to ChatWithAChaplain (http://www.healthcarechaplaincy.org/about-us.html). It is hard to keep up with what is developing in the field of pastoral/spiritual counseling and care. The kinetic nature of research is both exciting and challenging. During the week in which I began this chapter, I received two emails reflecting some of these changes and challenges. The first was an email from HealthCare Chaplaincy Network (HCCN) that featured a clip of actor William Christopher, aka Father Mulcahy of M*A*S*H speaking to HCCN. Many hold the image of Father Mulcahy as the image of a chaplain and understand chaplaincy in the context of what Father Mulcahy did. So it seemed serendipitous that this email came as I was looking to the future, because as good a chaplain as Father Mulcahy was, he does not represent where chaplaincy is heading now and in the future. In that same week I received an email from APC that was posted on its Linked In page asking what members thought about chaplaincy in a veterinarian's office. Anyone who has ever had to bring a sick pet to a vet to be euthanized knows what a difficult time that is and many might be comforted by a spiritual presence. Is it possible to integrate such dramatically disparate images, a military chaplain, and a veterinary chaplain, into current models?

As a Christian, I am reminded that many Christians hold the image of Christ as shepherd as a paradigm for ministry/pastoring even though most of us may not have a clue what shepherds do. More may only have seen live sheep in a zoo. Thinking a bit deeper about sheep and shepherds, many may not conclude that this is the proper image for spiritual ministry today. I have found that western, North American culture is prone to either/or thinking: either Father Mulcahy or the vet chaplain, not both Father Mulcahy and the vet chaplain.

My research revealed the following emerging themes:

- Increase in age of the chaplain, second or third career
- Increase in laity
- Increase in other faith traditions
- Change in where chaplaincy is done – expansion of the where- institution and world
- Increase in number of women in chaplaincy
- Change in what chaplaincy is called (spiritual care, interfaith chaplaincy)
- Increase in professionalization of the field, increase in requirements

During my five years of research and writing this book, two local Skilled Nursing Facilities called upon me as a consultant for hiring a new chaplain. They wanted to know about qualifications, pay scale, training, and just about anything related to chaplaincy. I spent hours with them explaining about chaplaincy, and they were both determined to put out an advertisement that included at least two units of CPE, (with the possibility of moving toward Board

Certification), and a graduate degree in theology (preferably Master of Divinity). They were both determined to get the most qualified chaplain available. In the end, they both hired who they thought was the best person for the job, and it was not someone who necessarily fulfilled their entire list of qualifications.

A third nursing home in town recently hired two new chaplains. They had numerous qualified, professionally trained, Board Certified Chaplain applicants. In the end, the decision on who to hire depended on who the Elders of the nursing home decided was the best fit and they hired two chaplains who had portions of what a Board Certified Chaplain has, but not everything. Clearly, although I understand and agree that education and professional training are very important components in becoming a professional chaplain, that alone does not make a good chaplain or guarantee employment. I completely support professional training and standards and have lived my life getting the requisite degrees and certifications. However, getting all those degrees and certifications alone is not what makes me a good professor and therapist. I have come to understand that values and attributes I bring to my work, my love of God and God's creation, my desire to be service-oriented, my years of experience, along with my many qualifications make me good at what I do.

Of course I want the chaplain to do no harm and to know what s/he is doing. However, in the 15 years I have trained volunteer hospice chaplains, not one dying person has asked about the credentials of the chaplain. I would suggest that perhaps there can be a distinction made in chaplaincy and that there can be pastoral or spiritual assistant chaplains. In the medical field we have Nurse Practitioners and Physician Assistants with differing education and requirements than physicians.

While finishing this book, in my other professional home, AAPC, where I currently serve as national Chair of Certification, dramatic changes are occurring. After August 1, 2015 no new applications for certification will be accepted. When I entered the field of pastoral counseling, I could not be credentialed despite all my training because I was a layperson; eventually I was able to be certified and now hold the status of Fellow. In the last 25 years, however, more and more states are requiring state licensure in order to counsel and less and less people are applying to be certified through AAPC. In the past, most pastoral and spiritual care providers followed the traditional path of M.Div., advanced clinical training, and another advanced degree, with lots of supervision. Now most applicants entering AAPC have acquired the clinical training, but not necessarily formal theological training, yet they wish to integrate spirituality with the counseling they do. In the last three years less than thirty people have applied to be certified – in any category - and the overall certified membership in AAPC has been reduced by almost half. Now each state defines who legally is a counselor, and what requirements are necessary to become one. In New York State one must be licensed as a psychotherapist, marriage and family therapist or mental health counselor. It seems to be that as pastoral counseling became more professionalized with requirements and wanting to be accepted in the secular world, pastoral counselors allowed themselves to sublimate or even lose their pastoral/spiritual identity. I would hate to see this happen in chaplaincy.

No amount of training can teach the most basic component of being a chaplain, minister or pastoral counselor– heart and compassion. Most of my students are over the age of 50 and are coming into ministry as a second or even third career. This model is typical of seminaries and graduate theological schools across the country. When these students come to me and say they want to be pastoral counselors, I have different advice for those younger than 50 and those 50 and older. It is the same with chaplaincy. I lay out what it would take to be a (pastoral) counselor or a chaplain that even with full-time study would take a number of years. I have one student who at the age of sixty-eight went to seminary full-time to get her M.Div. She will be ordained now at age seventy-one. Her heart is drawn to chaplaincy, and she was told that she needs to get a basic unit of CPE then do a residency and then more hours, and then apply to be Board Certified. Instead she is finding a way to do chaplaincy as part of her overall ministry so that she can do this while she can still walk!

Until 2006, New York State did not license Mental Health, Marriage and Family Therapists, or Psychotherapists, so I did not need a license or a particular degree to do pastoral counseling. I counseled with a M.Div., PhD, and AAPC certification, but many did not have these qualifications. In 2006 when the bill was passed for licensing it was decided that clergy could continue to do short-term counseling as part of their "charge." NY State did not want to interfere with any "church." However, those of us who are not ordained – despite our many years of education and training – had to be licensed by the state in order to continue doing counseling. I see a similar process-taking place in chaplaincy. Unless one is Board Certified, one cannot do chaplaincy. It does not seem to matter that one has a lifetime of experience, or is over sixty years of age, or that one has training and education. To be a chaplain requires being Board Certified.

In the time it has taken to have this book edited, reviewed and published, even more changes have occurred in the field:

- In 2015 PBS aired a documentary on Chaplains that showed chaplains of various faith traditions ministering in prisons, hospitals, medical centers, the armed forces, the Senate, NASCAR and a chicken processing plant
- In 2016 Health Care Chaplaincy Network formed the Spiritual Care Association, which broke from the traditional training of chaplains, and the 2004 Common Standards for Professional Chaplaincy and focused on evidence-based quality indicators, and a multi-disciplinary approach
- In 2017, five of the six Associations that produced the 2004 Common Standards produced the 2017 Common

Competencies for Professional Chaplains. A webinar explaining some key differences to the 2004 document can be found at http://ow.ly/OURp30bn7X6 as well as on the websites for APC/BCCI
- More programs are opening to train inter-faith chaplains, and here is less emphasis on having one Christian, denominational home

It is my hope that rather than saying the only way to be a chaplain is... we might say this pathway is the route to professional chaplaincy, but that we realize because of age, geographical, financial, or other challenges, not everyone can take this route and we will consider alternatives and equivalencies. What I hear in the world of CPE is similar to what I heard in the world of AAPC. To be a certified pastoral counselor, one must have an M.Div., be ordained, and be certified through AAPC. Given the reality of who wants to do chaplaincy, (lay people, second and third career, older adults, those not having an M.Div., those who want to do specialized chaplaincy – nursing home, hospice, veterinary clinics) - it is my hope for the future that there could be more flexibility in the requirements and training.

Comments from Terry R. Bard, Editor

Clearly, significant growth and many shifts in the field and practice of pastoral/spiritual care have evolved since the 1992 publication of Charles Hall's Head and Heart. New associations have sprouted, training models have matured, and interest in becoming a trained professional has expanded. Healthcare shifts have led to new professional opportunities particularly in long-term healthcare settings, hospice programs, and beyond. Furthermore, chaplaincy has become an important second and third career choice for men and women.

These many changes have simultaneously generated many

challenges. Once primarily hospital based, now Clinical Pastoral Education programs abound in a variety of settings including nursing homes, senior living organizations, and rehabilitation centers. CPE students may find clinical training opportunities in community centers, schools, the military, and locations other than medical institutions.

Currently, those entering the field present with backgrounds and profiles quite different from their forbears. Even as most clerical and seminary programs require students to take at least one unit of CPE, increasing numbers of laity now enroll in these programs. Formerly, most clinically trained pastoral care providers were ordained or invested clergy who regarded CPE to be a professional achievement of advanced training, often creating service and workplace opportunities outside the traditional models of church, synagogue, and the like. Consequently, professionally trained clergy could claim a specialty status and, with it, roles within institutions commensurate with other specialty trained care providers. Although not always the case, opportunities for leadership and service frequently evolved in the institutions in which they served.

As described throughout Body and Soul, the profile of the chaplain has evolved, expanding and changing significantly. Training associations such as ACPE and CPSP have been particularly successful in expanding their programs by expanding specialized training to laity. Doing so has been consistent with many social changes since the last quarter of the 21st century. In addition to the historical model of formal religious organizations and their institutions, the renewed interest in spirituality sometimes expressed outside of and beyond the prior formal models generated a new variety of models and settings. Evolving globalism contributed to societies identified by and expanding cultural pluralism and, with it, an increase of interfaith and inter-cultural families. Additionally, medical advances have enabled greater human life span so that many people live longer and remain active and healthy longer. New electronic opportunities, the worldwide web, social media, television options, and other developments have contributed to an awareness of greater varieties of belief systems generating increased religious and cultural syncretism. All of these shifts have contributed to how people look for and find meaning. In this context, the human searches for place and meaning have yielded novel alternatives quite different from traditional models.

This new context became a perfect setting for an evolution from formal religious models to a more amorphous claim on the human spirit. Nomenclature changes began to take place so that what once was called pastoral frequently became spiritual care. No longer were religious brands alone compelling. Chaplains became more adept in providing interfaith care than the specific denominational care of yesteryear. Training began to focus on interfaith care and, now, even this focus has evolved into spiritual care that is far more open to individual and cultural identities and wants. These shifts parallel current CPE training models and the many contexts from which those who seek to become chaplains or spiritual counselors come. Many of today's chaplains are no longer deeply grounded in the literature, traditions, and practices of particular faith traditions. They need not claim such connections nor do they need to concern themselves specifically with some of the transference and countertransference issues that formal clergy face.

These cultural changes and the expansion of chaplaincy credentials have altered the entire field. Many new CPE students, claiming one or two units of CPE, are now being hired as chaplains. Increasingly, these new chaplains are interfaith or sometimes simply spiritual. Though eager to learn, many are not well versed in religious or belief systems whether or not they profess or practice a formal religion or tradition. Interestingly, a recent very limited study suggests that fewer than expected numbers of these students advance to become board certified. Yet many become gainfully employed as chaplains.

Given the shifts in training, background, and context, those who enter chaplaincy as second or third careers constitute a cohort far different than those of earlier generations. Many new chaplains may have quite different professional, academic and financial expectations or needs of prior generations. Thus, they may seek less financial compensation and care less about professional advancement than those with more formal and advanced education and training. Simultaneously, the existing climate in which significant health care system shifts and financial limitations abound, the provision of less expensive chaplaincy care, if funds are available at all, offers an opportunity for this emerging model of chaplains and spiritual care providers.

It is difficult to predict what the next iterations of pastoral/spiritual care would look like. Societal shifts remain dynamic, but in the interim, it seems likely that the mid to late 20th century models of chaplaincy are likely to evaporate. Many health care organizations, particularly acute hospitals are currently reducing or eliminating formal CPE programs and pastoral/spiritual care departments. Increasingly, chaplains are more likely to be part-time or per diem employees or consultants who report to institutional departments such as nursing, social services, or activities directors. Greater opportunities for chaplains are more likely to be found in hospice, long-term care, rehabilitation, as well as other community settings such as fitness programs, schools, and, perhaps even in industry. How these new realities will shape pastoral/spiritual care associations and the educational and trainers and the training organizations remain elusive. The evolution from Head and Heart to Body and Soul will become archival resources for the next generation to write.

Works Cited

Accardi, Rod. "Happy Birthday to Us." Vision, Vol. 15, no. 7, July, 2005, pp. 2 and 9.

AAPC Member Application, 1992.

Augsburger, David W. Pastoral Counseling Across Cultures. Philadelphia: The Westminster Press, 1986.

Boisen, Anton. The Exploration of the Inner World. Philadelphia: University of Pennsylvania Press, 1971.

CASC/ACSS. Policy and Procedure Manual, ch. 2, section 1B. "Education Streams" and E. "Certification," 2013.

Dale, Diana. "Workplace Chaplaincy in the United States- History and Principles," unpublished document, 1992, rev. 2011.

De Jong, Jan. "Toward Indigenous CPE: A Mini-CPE Program at Grey's Hospital, Pietermaritzburg, KwaZulu-Natal." Reflective Practice: Formation and Supervision in Ministry. 2007, Volume 27, 2007, pp. 175-186.

DeVelder, John and Lawrence, Raymond J. "Guest Editorial: College of Pastoral Supervision and Psychotherapy Adds Its Sponsorship to The Journal of Pastoral Care & Counseling." The Journal of Pastoral Care & Counseling. Spring 2003, vol. 57, no. 1, pp. 1-2.

Egan, Gerard. The Skilled Helper: A Problem-Management and Opportunity-Development Approach to Helping. 9th edition. Belmont, CA.: Brooks/Cole, Cenage Learning, 2010.

Fitchett, George, Alexander Tartaglia, Diane Dodd-McCue and Patricia Murphy, "Educating Chaplains for Research Literacy: Results of a National Survey of Clinical Pastoral Education Residency Programs." Journal of Pastoral Care & Counseling." Vol. 66, no. 1, 2:1-11.

Gleason, John J. "The Congress on Ministry in Specialized Settings (COMISS): Quo Vadis?" The Journal of Pastoral Care. Summer 1993 vol. 47, no. 2, pp. 117-127.

Gleason, John J. "Guest Editorial: The Impact of Feminism on Clinical Pastoral Education." The Journal of Pastoral Care. Spring 1998 Vol. 52, no. 1, pp. 3-5.

Hall, Charles E. Head and Heart: The Story of the Clinical Pastoral Education Movement. Journal of Pastoral Care Publications, Inc., 1992.

Hemenway, Joan E. "Opening Up the Circle: Next Steps in Process Group Work in Clinical Pastoral Education (CPE)." The Journal of Pastoral Care and Counseling. Winter 2005 Vol. 59, no. 4, pp. 323-334.

Hunter, Rodney J., general editor. Dictionary of Pastoral Care and Counseling. Nashville: Abingdon Press, 1990.

Jernigan, Homer L. "Clinical Pastoral Education with Students from Other Cultures: The Role of the Supervisor." The Journal of Pastoral Care. Summer 2000, Vol. 54, no. 2, pp. 135-145.

Karaban, Roslyn A. "The Journey Home: Focus on Hospice Ministry." Ministry and Liturgy, February 2006, pp. 14-16.

Kwon, Soo-Young and Duc Le, Anthony. "Relationship Building in Clinical Pastoral Education: A Confucian Reflection from Asian Chaplains." The Journal of Pastoral Care and Counseling, Fall 2004, vol. 58, no. 3, pp. 203-214.

Lartey, Emmanuel. "Globalization, Internationalization, and Indigenization of Pastoral Care and Counseling," in Nancy J. Ramsay, ed. Pastoral Care and Counseling: Redefining the Paradigms. Nashville: Abingdon Press, 2004.

Lawrence, Raymond J. "Eleventh CPSP Plenary Meeting Report to the Community," March 15, 2001.

Little, N. Keith. "Clinical Pastoral Education as Professional Training: Some Entrance, Curriculum and Assessment Implications." The Journal of Pastoral Care & Counseling, Fall/Winter 2010, vol. 64. No. 3: 5:1-8.

Massey, Kevin "Surfing Through a Sea Change: The Coming Transformation of Chaplaincy Training." Reflective Practice: Formation and Supervision in Ministry, 2014, vol. 34, 144-152.

Miller-McLemore. "Revisiting the Living Human Web." The Journal of Pastoral Care and Counseling, Spring-Summer, 2008. Vol. 62, nos. 1-2, pp. 3-18.

Pontifical Congregations and Council Staffs. "Instruction on Certain Questions Regarding the Collaboration of the Nonordained Faithful in the Sacred Ministry of Priests." August 15, 1997.

Tartaglia, Alexander, George Fitchett, Diane Dodd-McCue, Patricia Murphy, and Paul Derrickson, "Teaching Research in Clinical

Pastoral Education: A Survey of Model Practices." Journal of Pastoral Care & Counseling, March 2013, vol. 67:1, 5:1-14.

Tartaglia, Alexander E. "Reflections on the Development and Future of Chaplaincy Education." Reflective Practice: Formation and Supervision in Ministry, 2015, vol. 35, 116-133.

Thornton, Edward E. Professional Education for Ministry. Nashville: Abingdon Press, 1970.

United States Conference of Catholic Bishops. Co-Workers in the Vineyard of the Lord. Washington D.C.: USCCB, 2005.

VandeCreek, Larry and Burton, Laurel., eds. "Professional Chaplaincy: Its Role and Importance in Healthcare." The Journal of Pastoral Care. Spring 2001, vol. 55, no. 1, pp. 81-97.

VanKatwyck, Peter. "What to Communicate: A New Chapter in Pastoral Care and Counseling?" The Journal of Pastoral Care. Fall 2000, Vol. 54, no. 3, pp. 243-252.

Willis, R. Wayne. "Guest Editorial: To What Shall We Liken the Hospital Chaplain?" The Journal of Pastoral Care. Winter 1999, vol. 53, no. 4, pp. 391-394.

Websites consulted:

> http://www.nacc.org/certificationdefault.aspx
> http://www.urmc.rochester.edu/chaplaincy/CPE/programs.cfm
> http://www.allinahealth.org/ahs.cpe.nst/page/cpe_programs
> http://www.carolinashealthcare.org/clinical-pastoral-education-programs
> http://s531162813.onlinehome.us/faq/
> http://www.merriam-webster.com/dictionary/chaplain?show=0&t=1389281146

http://comissnetwork.org
http://www.acpe.edu/?m=2518
http://s531162813.onlinehome.us/mission-and-vision-html
http://s531162813.online.us/about
http://acpe.edu/WhoWeAreRR.html
http://www.najc.org/about/history
http://www.professionalchaplains.org/content.asp?contentid=24
http://www.pastoralreport.com/covenant.html
http://www.pastoralreport.com/The Standards of CPSP 2013-5.pdf
http://www.spiritualcare.ca/index.asp
http://www.spiritualcare.ca/page.asp?ID=157
http://www.spiritualcare.ca/researchdetails.asp?ID=138
http:/work.chron.com/requirements-become-army-chaplain-14316.html
http://www.nibic.com/703033
http://www.correctionalchaplains.org/what_is_the_acca.htm
www.IPFCA.org
http://ipfca.org/membership
http://ipfca.org/about
http://www.acpe.edu/NewPDF/2010%20_Manuals/2010%/20 Standards.pdf
http://www.muslimchaplains.org/about-us/history
http://www.muslimschaplains.org/aboutus/faq
www.nacc.org/docs/resources/NACC-Evolution%520of%20
http://www.professionalchaplains.org/Files/professional_standards/common_standards_professional_chaplaincy.pdf
(http://www.healthcarechaplaincy.org/about-us.html
http://acpe.edu
http://www.acpe.edu/DirectoriesDortedE.html
http://acpe.edu/DirectoriesInternationalAffiliates.html
http://www.healthcarechaplaincy.org/about-us.html
http://www.healthcarechaplaincy.org/about-us.html
http://ow.ly/OURp30n7X6

Emails:

May 13, 2015 email from David Lichter, NACC
August 14, 2014 email from Cecille Asekoff, NAJC
August 20, 2013 email from Sharon Sheflett, AAPC
August 26, 2013 email from Karen McCray, AAPC
May 19, 2015 email from David Lichter, 2015
August 26, 2013 email from Philip Paradowski, NACC
October 9 and October 13, 2013 emails from Cecille Asekoff, NAJC
March 26, 2015 email from Carol Pape, APC
September 17 and October 8, 2013 emails from Diane Gerard, APC
November 20, 2013 email from Toni Sedfawi, CASC/ACSS

The Clinical Pastoral Education movement is a story without end.... The challenge was to get beyond the mass of data to sort and organize the materials. The story could easily be overwhelmed by historical data; missing the forest on account of the trees. In an attempt to lighten the process the book follows a simple sequence of one word headings: What, Who, Where, How, When and Wherefore. This organization is engaging as it found a place for a multitude of recorded events yet manages to maintain a narrative format and focus on the larger picture patterns and themes.

Peter L. Van Katwyk
Professor Emeritus
Waterloo Lutheran Seminary
Waterloo, ON, Canada

Body and Soul offers an important narrative of the scholarship on and the practice of clinical pastoral education in the U.S. over the last 25 years. Prof. Karaban portrays the complex and divisive history of the movement and reveals both the threats to and the accomplishments of the discipline. Body and Soul fills a significant gap in the literature and its organization makes the book easily readable and interesting.

Rev. Jill L. Snodgrass, Ph.D.
Loyola University Maryland

www.ingramcontent.com/pod-product-compliance
Lightning Source LLC
Chambersburg PA
CBHW032007080426
42735CB00007B/537